Who Is My Neighbor?

Who Is My Neighbor?

Life Experiences of Immigrants and Refugees

Edited by
Warren and Margaret Roth

Editing and composition: Thomas P. Fenton/WorldViews
Cover graphic credit: Photograph by Roger Libman of a ceramic by Kim Acera. Courtesy: People's Resource Center.

ISBN-13: 978-1501018893
ISBN-10: 1501018892

Contents

Foreword

Who Is My Neighbor?

This book is about neighbors, special neighbors, those who have come to us from afar and whom we have met through the People's Resource Center (PRC) in Wheaton, Illinois. As part of a project called Life Experiences, the PRC is bringing to you the stories of some of those who have become part of the PRC community. Most of the accounts contained in this book are by people who came to DuPage County from countries in Africa, Asia, and Latin America either as refugees or as immigrants. They are clients and volunteers and have agreed to share their stories so that all of us at the PRC and the larger local community can get a better understanding of who our neighbors are, the problems they have faced, and what they have accomplished in their lives. We interviewed people from nineteen countries: Africa: Ethiopia, Liberia, Sierra Leone, South Sudan, Sudan, Tanzania; Asia: Afghanistan, Bhutan, China, Iran, Iraq, Myanmar (Burma), Sri Lanka, Vietnam; Latin America: Chile, Colombia, Mexico. Europe: Germany; and the United States.

The Life Experiences Project is a development of the Story Telling Project begun in the Art Department of the PRC in 2008 under the supervision of Rosie Dixon. Kim Perez, executive director of the PRC asked the editors to revive this project in 2013. The present project is a joint effort with Benedictine University. Five history students from Benedictine University were the interviewers for most of the life histories in this book. Under the guidance of the editors, Margaret and Warren Roth, the students have worked around their own class and employment schedules and the time constraints of those they interviewed. They each encountered interviewees who are from different countries and are in the process of learning English as a second language. The students have submitted written copies of the interviews and the editors have had their interviewees read, correct, and sign off on the version that appears in this book.

The object of compiling these life histories is to give you, the reader, a better understanding of the neighbors you meet when you come to the People's Resource Center, and in your own neighborhood in DuPage County. In most (but not all) cases, the names of those who agreed to be interviewed have been changed because political conditions in their home countries are unsettled and many still have family members living in those countries. All those interviewed, however, have agreed to allow the PRC to publish their stories. Some PRC clients, however, even after years in the United States, are still worried that anything they say could negatively affect family members at home. Their fear is so deep that they decided not to have their stories published after they saw them in writing.

The editors hope that this work will be the first of a series of volumes of life stories that will become an ongoing history of the PRC as told through the lives of clients, volunteers, staff, and supporters of the organization. In other words, we look forward to a continuing answer to the question that is our title, "Who Is My Neighbor?"

Editors: Margaret and Warren Roth
Student interviewers: Chris Caballero, Victoria Harwood, Rachel Jones, Sadia Mohiuddin, Jason Vitell
Benedictine University coordinator of the Internship Course: Dr. Vincent Gaddis, chair of the Department of History, Philosophy and Religious Studies

Our special thanks to all those who have consented to share a part of the stories of their lives. They have strengthened the community that is the People's Resource Center because to know one another and to care for one another is what community is all about. The editors hope that as you read these life experiences and better understand the difficulties our neighbors have overcome you will see difficulties in your own life in a new and more hopeful light.

Special thanks also go to MaryAnna Milton, director of the Family Literacy Program, who was our contact person at the PRC. She suggested most of the interviewees. She made endless phone calls, helped with the arrangements of appointment dates, and helped get the necessary consent of the interviewees. Kim Perez, executive director of the PRC, read the first draft of the manuscript and provided many helpful corrections. Tutors/teachers/translators John Argyrakis, Pat Bernhold, Barbara Filipski, Peter Kanjama, Ron Mertzlufft, Robert Russo, and Diane Rodriguez also provided names and/or sat in on some interviews and helped with the consent forms. Adriana Bautista, Nicole Love, Kathy Richardson, and Sanjuana Rodriguez made all the room assignments for the interviews, a difficult task at the very busy and crowded PRC. Pam Knight, Vince Fagin, and Luciano Rodriguez helped to find interviewees. Without all of them, this project would not have been possible.

Our thanks also go to Vince Gaddis, who selected the students and supervised the academic part of the internship, and Julie Wroblewski, Archives and Special Collection Librarian at Benedictine University, who gave the students an overview on how to prepare for and conduct a life experience interview.

❑

Introduction

Our neighbors have come as immigrants and as refugees (see definitions p. 12 below) and they have come for a wide variety of reasons. The important fact is that they are our neighbors and getting to know them means getting to know their histories. The parts of their lives they have been willing to share with us are not complete autobiographies, but they do give us an insight into their reasons for coming and the hardships they have endured as well as the successes they have had. Their stories vary in length and intensity but all are "real life."

The interviewers were asked to write what they heard in the first person so that you, the reader, might feel that you were listening to a live person sitting across from you. The interviewers were also asked to write up the interviews, as far as possible, in the style of the person speaking. For this reason, the interviews will differ from one another not only in content but in the way they come across. In some cases, the subjects touched upon by the interviewees mirror the anguish and disruption they felt as they fled conflict and danger in their homelands, in others cases, fear for family left behind in the countries from which they came. A number put great emphasis on the education they were not able to get before they came to the United States but were able to get after they arrived. In all cases, regardless of content or style, there is sincerity and the strong desire to let you, the reader, know what their lives have been.

As editors, we have had two main objectives: to maintain the integrity of the original interview and to make each interview transcript as readable as possible. To those ends, we have assigned fictitious names to many of the interviewees because they or their families could possibly be endangered by what they told the interviewers. We have also left out names of hometowns where we felt this information might compromise identities. Again, as editors we deleted obvious repetition and we corrected grammar where an error would obscure the meaning of what the interviewee was trying to get across. We were careful, however, to keep the tone and the emotion that the interviewer experienced. That is why we have added short introductions and, in some instances, "editors' notes" to the interviews.

About the interviews themselves. Most were done by the Benedictine University students mentioned in the Foreword. The editors also did some of the interviews. All the interviews have been read and signed by the interviewees to make sure that they contained what the interviewee wanted told. Scheduling and bringing the interviewers and interviewees together at times presented a challenge to all concerned. Everyone had time constraints and at least one that had to be cut short in one location was later continued in a restaurant. All the interviews were done in English except for one that was conducted in Urdu. Most were conducted at the People's Resource Center and in some cases tutors from the PRC who had worked closely with the interviewees sat in on the interview. Since each Benedictine student had to do five interviews, one of the editors sat in on at least one interview for each student. Finally, the students were required by their faculty director, Dr. Vincent Gaddis, to write a lengthy reflection on what they had gained from the interviewing experience. Excerpts from those reflections are included in the final notes in this book.

We have divided the interviews into five groupings based on the themes that the interviewees stressed. Some of the interviews contain more than one of these themes, but, in most cases, one theme predominates. The themes are:

Victims of War
Victims of Discrimination
Family Considerations
Economic Considerations
Volunteers

All interviews mention the role of the People's Resource Center in the interviewees' life in the United States. Two of the accounts are by volunteers who have had extensive international experience and one is the story of a woman who came to the PRC as a client and then became a volunteer and later a staff member.

For some of the interviews, we have added postscripts where an interviewee attained a milestone, such as citizenship, after the interview was given.

The interviewed clients and the volunteers are connected with the PRC's Empowerment Programs. Almost all of them are members of the Family Literacy Program. Some are studying or helping others prepare for the GED or for the citizenship test; others simply wanted to be able to read and write in English. Many of them are also taking computer classes and some are involved with the Art Program. They have all expressed a strong desire to better their English in order to become more integrated into U.S. society and to get better jobs.

This book is, in a very real way, a second installment of the history of the PRC that was begun in *Miracles Relied Upon: A History of the People's Resource Center* (2012). *Who Is My Neighbor?* is not a complete history because it does not give the life experiences of every client, volunteer, and staff member. It does, however, present the reader with a view of the lives of a special category of those whose lives have been touched and changed by the PRC. As editors, we hope that the life experiences of other clients, volunteers, and staff members will be recorded because their stories are the ongoing history of the PRC community.

Difference between Immigrants and Refugees

Refugees generally do not leave their home countries voluntarily. When they do, they often have to spend years in a United Nations refugee camp where a lottery or an interview system assigns them to different countries. The UN and the accepting countries determine that they cannot go back to their own countries, either because of war, political, religious or ethnic persecution, or economic discrimination. Once the U.S. government grants refugee status to a person, that person has immediate legal standing upon entry into the country and has an easier time to become a citizen (once their English is good enough that they can pass the citizenship test). Refugees generally have endured poverty in their own country and in refugee camps in neighboring countries to which they fled, and they enter the United States with no possessions. They are assigned apartments and many have sponsors who help them with daily expenditures till they can find a job. If they are over the age of retirement, they receive a small stipend (SSI) from the U.S. government. This is generally not enough to pay for all expenses, and they have to rely on agencies like the PRC for extra food, clothing, and education.

Refugees miss their countries—they did not come voluntarily—and they cannot go home. Their biggest regret is that they cannot help the families they had to leave at home. Refugees come for various reasons, but mainly because of political and economic upheaval and hardships such as war, torture, or deaths of family members or because of discrimination due to their ethnic or religious background.

Immigrants, by contrast, leave their home countries voluntarily, usually for economic reasons. They come legally, but do not receive any government support; or they come as undocumented and try to become legal residents and eventually citizens. Immigrants come from all economic classes.

Immigrants feel that they have a choice to go back and help their families. They come mainly to better their economic lives or because of personal and family conflicts. Some immigrants come with or later bring other family members. While some immigrants were rather well off in their countries, the majority lived in poverty in rural areas with scant basic services

Educational levels range from no schooling to some college-level education. People who are now learning to read and write English never went to school before and may not be able to read or write their own language. Some had never ridden in a car before arriving at a refugee camp. Very few of the interviewees knew how to drive a car. This was a major problem in DuPage County.

❑

Victims of War

The people whose stories appear in this section all have first-hand experience of war in their home countries. They have lived in fear of bodily harm to themselves and their loved ones, and they have known what it means to flee from their homes with little or nothing of their personal possessions. Worse still, they have suffered the heartbreak of separation from family members, especially parents from children.

As if war were not enough, they have spent days and, in some cases, months getting to places of relative safety only to find a whole new set of hardships in refugee camps. Though safe from the violence of actual warfare, they experienced hunger, lack of health and sanitary facilities, and the constant fear of exploitation by those who run the camps and from fellow refugees. All the time, they lived in a state of uncertainty about how long they would have to stay in the camp and if they would ever be able to return to their own homes. Some returned to their home country after the political situation had changed in their host country; some of the returnees were forced to leave their country once again. Theirs is an odyssey that lasted till they reached the United States.

Finally, they have felt the roller coaster ride of joy and disappointment as they applied for asylum and were forced to endure the bureaucratic nightmare of filling out forms, going to interviews, and waiting for long periods only to find that not all of their family would be able to leave the camp together.

Those who have suffered from war always carry the memories of violence and their escape from it. In some cases, they continue to seek family members from whom they have been separated for many years.

❑

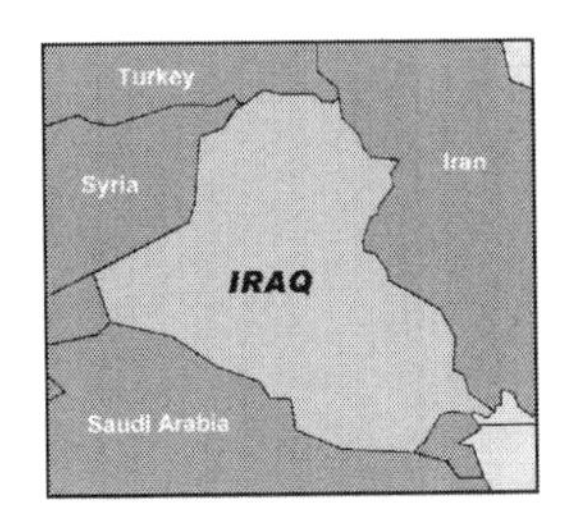

Charles D.

Interviewed, Spring 2014

I am a 75-year-old man. I was born in Iraq's capital of Baghdad in 1938. Because of the violence and political unrest in Iraq, with sorrow, my wife and my daughter first left Iraq for Amman, Jordan, and my two sons and I followed them. My older brother lives in Amman because his wife is Jordanian. They gave my family and me a place to live. By profession, I am an accountant and I speak English as well as Arabic. I am also a Catholic Christian.

The Iraq I remember as a boy was very different than it is now. People of all nationalities and religions lived together in my district of Baghdad in peace. There were Arabs, both Shiites and Sunnis, as well as Kurds, Jews, and Christians. I went to a high school run by Jesuit priests who treated all the boys equally, whether they were Christians or not. It was there that I learned English. After I became an accountant, I worked for private companies and for the Iraqi government. Because I spoke English well, I started working as an accountant for a British company that had an office in Baghdad.

I built a house in the central district of Baghdad in 1974, and this is where my children were born. As a Christian I felt safe because I was not a member of a political party. Most Christians did not get involved in politics. But my house was in a good place, close to the presidential palace, and one day I got a letter from the government requesting me to leave my house. This was before the Americans invaded Iraq. I think they wanted me to move because government people wanted my house, which was near the president's palace. Then the Americans came and in March 2003 my house was destroyed by a shell from an American tank. I was not in the house, but I saw it happen, and the American officer in the tank came and said that he was sorry that he had to destroy the house because he was getting resistance from people in the house. I was able to stay with other relatives in Iraq, but after the war, there was no security in Iraq and there was electricity for only two or three hours a day. That is why I took my family to Jordan. My wife and daughter were able to enter Jordan right away, but my sons and I had to wait to get entry permits and we were very worried that we might not be allowed to enter, because the Jordanian government was afraid that males were politically active. Finally, I believe, because we were Christians, we were allowed to enter Jordan. However, since we had refugee status, I was not allowed to work.

In 2009, my family and I decided to leave Jordan. One of my sons went to Holland as a refugee, and my wife, daughter, and other son came with me to the United States. We had relatives in Westmont, Illinois, who sponsored us, and the United Nations helped us to enter the United States.

I had no trouble coming to the United States. Even though I am seventy-five, I was able to get a job at Jewel and make some money. My daughter got married and went to England. My son is an electrical engineer, but the only job he could get in the United States was a night job in a Target store, even though he has his masters degree from New York University's school in Amman.

I have my Green Card so that I can stay in the United States, and I am coming to the People's Resource Center to get ready to take my citizenship examination. My tutor is helping me greatly, but I hear that it is very difficult to pass the citizenship examination now.

I am very happy in the United States because I do not see the religious differences that made me leave Iraq. But I would go back to Iraq if things change there.

❑

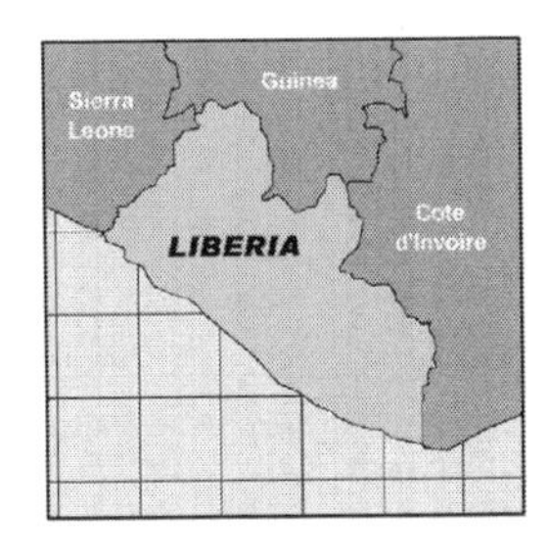

Karen C.

Interviewed, Spring 2014

I was born in a small village outside of Monrovia, Liberia, West Africa, in 1984. When I was six years old, civil war began in Liberia and I spent two weeks with my family hiding in the bush to survive. My mother had ten children, two died as babies and four died in the civil war. One of my sisters is much older than I am, and I grew up with her taking the place of my mother.

The civil war was going on as my sister and I got out of Liberia and got to a refugee camp in Ivory Coast. We spent many years in the camp and I was not able to go to school. I could not learn to read and write, but I did learn some French. I understand some French now but I cannot speak it.

While we were in the refugee camp, my sister was able to buy some land and we could grow food for ourselves and sold some to others in the camp. The camp was very large and it took my sister and me a long time to find my mother and two brothers, who had also left Liberia because of the civil war. We had a house in the camp, but sometimes we went back to living in a tent. My life as a child was hard. Once, when the rain made the river run very fast, I fell in. It was my sister's husband, who I considered my father, who saved me. Another time, I fell in a well while I was getting water and I had to be saved again. We all had to do chores and if we did not do them we were beaten. I was also sexually abused more than once while I lived in the camp.

The Red Cross ran the camp and it was World Relief Services that got us out of the camp and to the United States. We went from the camp to Abidjan, the capital of Ivory Coast. For two years, we all had to have interviews, many interviews, and they always asked the same questions to see if we were telling the truth. When the interviews were over, we waited for a letter with our picture on it. If the letter came with a picture, it meant that we would go to the United States. My sister and one of her sons and I were picked, but many of our friends were not picked, and we were sad about that.

We had to have a sponsor to come to the United States and our sponsor family gave us a place to stay until we could get into an apartment. It was January 2004 when we came. I was happy to come to the United States because my mother was already here. It was the first time that I could sleep in a bed with pillows and sheets. The year after I came, I spent three months in a hospital with cancer. I am now a cancer survivor.

When I arrived at O'Hare Airport, I could not read the signs because I could not read and write. I started a course in English as a Second Language at Wheaton College. This was the first time in my life that I was in a real school. I then came to PRC to continue to study English with a tutor. I am getting ready to take my citizenship examination next year. I now have two children who are American citizens. I like it here because I am not afraid of war and what happened in the camp. But I would like to go back to Liberia to see the place where I was born.

Editors' note: When Karen signed her story for release, she added: "I took my citizenship test and passed. So, I am now a U.S. citizen."

❑

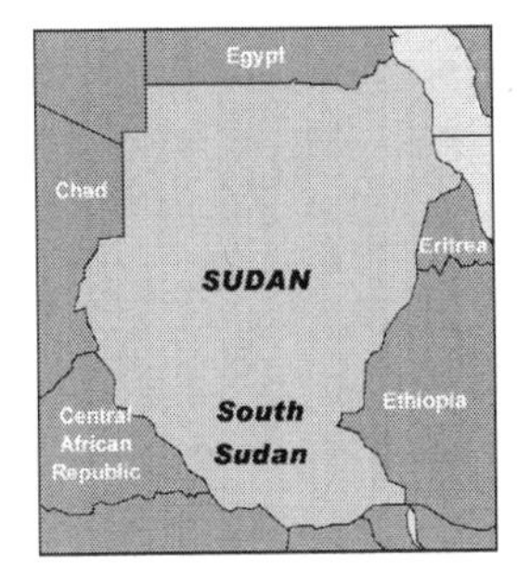

Arkangelo Piot

Interviewed, 2008 and Spring 2014

Editors' note: Arkangelo is a young man who was born in what was then the country of Sudan in northeastern Africa. He became part of a group of seven- to fifteen-year-olds who were forced to flee their homes because of civil war. They became known as the "Lost Boys of Sudan." Their flight took them into Ethiopia, back to Sudan, and finally to Kenya. A documentary about their struggles and long march, *God Grew Tired of Us*, has been seen by many. The book *What Is the What: The Autobiography of Valentino Achak Deng,* by Dave Eggers about the boys was a finalist in the National Book Critics Award in 2006. When asked if he had read the book, Arkangelo said, "the book is about a friend of mine, and everything that happened to him in Sudan happened to me too."

I was born in what is now South Sudan, East Africa, and I am a Dinka by ethnicity. We were not born in hospitals so there were no records of our birth. We knew what year we were born, based on an event that took place the year we were born. When I came to the United States, we were told you could not live in the United States without knowing the record of your birth, so we were allowed to choose the year. I decided to choose September 28, 1976. Most of our Lost Boys were given January 1, but when I was in Kenya, one of my girlfriends was born 9/28. She used to celebrate her birthday, so I decided to do that together with her.

Attack on his village led to trek to Ethiopia

I was about nine-years-old when the trouble started, but before that, we were living with our father. The village was really a peaceful place. In the village in which we lived, there were mostly close relatives. We used to play outside because we didn't go to school. We had to take care of the cattle, goats, and sheep, because our relatives were farmers. That's the work of the boy, to look after the goat or cattle. If you are not doing that, you are playing outside with your friends. So when the trouble started, some of us were outside taking care of the cattle and others were in the village.

People who were attacking our village were the government-supported militia groups that used to fight against the rebels, called SPLA (Sudan People's Liberation Army). They were protecting us and fighting the militia and the government. They were mainly from South Sudan and ethnic Dinka and Nuer. The militia groups were mostly Arabs, who were supplied with everything including weapons by the Sudanese government in Khartoum. There were different attacks at different times. They came day or night. Our relatives told us, "When you hear something, don't come back to the village. Maybe something happened when you were away; you might find that everybody ran away already from the village. You will get attacked in the village."

They used to take and kill kids and grown-ups. They would take the older boys for slavery. One of my close friends was taken, with the family, all of them, mother and other children. The day I left, the village was all burned down, and I spent the night away. In the morning, I found some people moving east. They were from different villages and some from the same village I came from. I didn't know where we were going at that time, because the village was burned down and many people had been killed. I was with that group and just followed them. We moved like that for three months to Ethiopia. We didn't walk during the day, because if the government troops found you, they would start shooting. The reason they killed people moving was because they knew there were rebels from Southern Sudan in Ethiopia who were training people to come back and fight. So, when they found a group of people moving, they imagined that these people were the ones who were being trained.

Sometimes when they got some little boys, and didn't see a big man with them, they didn't kill them. Instead, they asked, "Where is your father. Is your father in Bilfam [a training camp in Ethiopia]?" We didn't know what Bilfam or Ethiopia was. Some of the questioners would speak Arabic, and they had translators that they had captured who could speak a little Arabic and Dinka. The little boys didn't know anything. Sometimes they would just point their hands in the direction where they were running. The militia was looking for men who would be in the SPLA, so they asked, "Why is your father not here?" They knew if they came back from Ethiopia they would come back as a soldier. So, if they saw you, they had to shoot and kill you. There are towns on the way to Ethiopia. If the militia saw a group of people moving, they sent troops out to see who these people were. We used to move at night, and when it was morning, we rested under a tree. Also during the day, people got thirsty. For these two reasons, we used to move at night.

The night was also dangerous. Lions and hyenas used to move at night looking for food. We had problems with this. The majority of us were boys, from five- to thirteen-years-old. These we considered adults who took care of us. When we walked at night, we used to walk in a single line of about nine or ten boys, the one in front was the one leading us, and the one in back was the one making sure nothing happened. When something happened, like a lion attacked, they had us sit down. They told us not to run away, because if we did, we would be giving the lion a chance to get us alone. That is why they made that line.

They used to tell us that when we reached Ethiopia we would have everything. Some of us died along the way, because there was no medicine or food. Others died due to diarrhea. We were drinking water from the rivers, and at the time, we didn't know what caused the diarrhea. When one of us died, they would tell us that somebody had died here, and if we didn't continue to walk we would be dead like them. That's how they used to encourage us until we reached Ethiopia. The first thing we realized when we got there was that there was nothing there.

We met different people coming from different villages and that made our group larger. When we reached Ethiopia, the number of boys was about 27,000. We came from different places, and we didn't move at the same time, so we didn't arrive at the same time. Our group was the second one to arrive at that place. Many groups came after us. We didn't know each other and didn't even speak the same languages. There are many languages in Sudan. We didn't know where we were going when we got there. So the time we were there, especially at the beginning, was really difficult. We spent about six months, with lots of problems.

First, there were some people who came to see us. I don't know who they were. That time, I still remember we were taught a song of welcome. We sang that song, but I don't know the meaning of the song, because we didn't know English. We were just told there were people coming to see us, and they were from America. At that time, I didn't know what America was or where it was. A teacher taught us to sing the song, "Welcome, welcome American Congressman." When these visitors arrived, it was the first time for me to see a white person. I didn't know there were white people around. I didn't know there were people of a different color. So, the white people came, and we welcomed them. We were so surprised to see somebody with a different color. We were trying to touch them. I wanted to feel the skin, but I didn't make it to reach them. I didn't know anything about that color.

So, when these people went back to America, we started getting food. We were told by the teachers, "These people are from the United Nations and are from America." When they went back to America, we started going on with life. We were getting food and medicine. They built a clinic for us so we could go there when we got sick.

We started going to school and started writing A, B, C, D, on the ground, because there were no books for our writing exercises. When they were able to give us these books, there were not enough, so one book was shared by two people. We had to cut them into two pieces. After two years, everybody got their own exercise books. They were teaching us English and Arabic. Arabic was not introduced as much as English. There were a lot of teachers there to teach us English.

We lived in Ethiopia for four years, and then the trouble started again. The Ethiopian government changed; it was overthrown by rebels. When the government that accommodated us was overthrown, the new government did not want to take care of us.

Fleeing from Ethiopia back to Sudan

The new government was training in northern Sudan. So they were not our friends. They came looking for us. When they came into power, they started coming to the refugee camp. So we ran away from Ethiopia, and everybody ran back to Sudan. When we ran to Sudan, we ran into a difficult problem. There was a river, the Gilo, to cross. We ran away in May, and May is the rainy season, and the river overflowed. To cross the river, we were using two boats. When I say a boat, I mean a wooden boat that holds like nine people. These two boats were not enough for all boys. We were chased by the troops from Ethiopia, but had to wait for some days to cross this river. The government then realized everybody had moved from the camp. They got out on the river and started shooting people. Everybody who was on the riverbank jumped in the river even though they didn't know how to swim. A number of the boys drowned there. There was another problem; there were crocodiles in the river. So many died there, either killed by bullets, crocodiles, or by drowning. So, we lost like three or four thousand in a single day.

We came to Pochalla, a town on the border of Sudan and Ethiopia. When we got there, the SPLA was there. They welcomed us, but told us that we could not go where they were living. They allowed us to live in a distant village. We stayed in Pochalla from May 1991 to 1992. There was no way we could get food until the Red Cross came in August and started bringing food. While we were there, in July, there was no food, and it was raining all the time. In July, a group of journalists came. They were from somewhere else; not the U.S. They searched everywhere and were asking the boys what had happened and what we were eating. That time was really terrible. There was no food and some boys looked so bad you could not recognize them as human beings. When the journalists came there, they were really surprised to see how people were living. They had interviewed some boys there and had taped some boys as they were talking to them. One of the teachers said, "Come now and listen to BBC News." We heard one of the Lost Boys reading a book on BBC. That was the end of July and then in August they started bringing food. They dropped it from airplanes. There also was still a problem with the government of Sudan. They were sending people to come and drop bombs on us. It was good, though, because it was the rainy season and the bombs would drop into the muck and not explode. They knew we were in Pochalla, so they came there. It was not easy, but God helped that time, because when the bombs dropped down they didn't explode. It only killed you if it was dropped on you.

When the dry season came, we were told we were to move away from there, because once the rainy season was over, the militias would come and get us. I left Pochalla in February of 1992. We left because there was no food and it was the dry season. When it is the dry season there is no water. The river dries up. But the main reason we left is because we were attacked by the Sudanese government, which captured the town two days after we left. We heard that news when we were on the way. We were told that these people could follow the road and find us. They had vehicles, and we were still walking. So we had to move again, but the ones who were in the hospital or couldn't walk were captured. They took them, and I don't know what happened to them.

When we left Pochalla, we went to Narus, a town in Sudan. Nearby was a town called Kapoeta, which was captured by the SPLA. This was a mile away from where we were living. In May 1992 that place was recaptured by the Sudanese government. We were told Kapoeta had been captured by the government army, and we didn't know what might happen. They were using trucks when they came to this place. We were told in the evening. Our teacher called out, and I was playing soccer outside that day. They told us, "Everybody, come here. We are leaving here now. Kapoeta has been captured and the Sudanese army could arrive here anytime."

The boys flee again from Sudan, this time to Kenya

At that point, we didn't count the boys. I don't know the number. In Narus, when we were told we were going to leave, the United Nations was negotiating with Kenya so the Kenyan government would allow us to enter. They had not come to an agreement. When they captured Kapoeta, we did not wait for permission to enter Kenya. That place was very far, but we made it in one day, because we were afraid of what was behind us. I was one of the first people to arrive there. I spent the whole night walking. At 1 P.M., we arrived in Kenya.

The Kenyan police were stopping people there. When the number of people got bigger, they were searching people, thinking we came in with guns. Some spent two days on route to Kenya. By the time we arrived in Lokichokio, on May 25, the Kenyan government was in control of that town. This was on the border, and there was some fighting between local people in Lokichokio and Sudan. They used to have a problem, because they are cattle keepers and those from Sudan came and raided the cattle of the Kenyans.

They agreed to take us to Kakuma. That time was a good trip, because it was arranged. They used a big truck. Nobody was walking. That was the first time for me to be in a truck. We rode from Lokichokio to Kakuma. The good thing was that we were in that truck, but it wasn't a good time. Everybody was sick. When we were told we were to get into the truck, we didn't know trucks took a certain number of people. The driver tried to reduce the number, but some were standing and some were sitting down. People were suffering from motion sickness.

We arrived at Kakuma on August 21. We started living there, and then they started putting in water pumps. So, we lived in Kakuma until we started coming to the United States. For me, I was there from 1992 to 2005. I have been here for nine years. Some of the boys were due to come in 2001, but due to September 11th, we were delayed. A lot of their paperwork got lost.

When the immigration agencies started listing people, there was a problem. They had some lawyers from the United States go and interview the boys. The program had been organized by the United Nations and the U.S. government. So when they interviewed with the lawyers, they knew all the stories of the boys. They asked, "How did you come here? What is your name?" There are some names that didn't appear. Maybe your name appeared two times and then disappeared. There was a problem with the Kenyan people. They were the ones working with us and with the UN. They used the names for someone else to come to the United States. They would sell the names to different people. This process was for the Lost Boys only, but there were some other people living there in the camp who were not Lost Boys. If they had money, they paid someone to give you the name of a Lost Boy which would allow you to emigrate. The people in charge sold the names. Some of the boys' names didn't appear. In our group alone, three people are still in Africa. We don't know what happened, because they did the interview, but their names didn't appear.

When I was in the camp, Catholic Relief sponsored some of us to go to Nairobi so we could get an education. I applied when I was in Kakuma in 1999 and was accepted to study there. I was in school in Nairobi at the time the lottery process started. During this time, a friend wrote that my name came up for me to leave, but since I was in Nairobi, I could not afford the bus to come back, and the school told me: "No, we don't have enough money for you to go to the camp.," because the sister who ran our school had told the United Nations: "I have some Lost Boys here. They're here with me in school. I don't have enough money to send them during the process. Now they are done with their training. I don't have jobs to employ them. I don't have money to keep them; nothing." The United Nations said they had our names and were going to screen to see which ones were the Lost Boys. The United Nations knew there were some with those names already. They would say, "This name has been used already by somebody to go to the United States, so we are not going to accept them." So, I told my friend I couldn't make it, because there was no money for me to go there. He said, "If you don't come, maybe you are going to miss it." I told him to take my name or just forget about it because there was no way. So he waited for like three weeks and sent me a letter and said my name was on the board again. I told him, "No, I can't come. Just take that name. Use it. There is no way I can come there." His name was still on hold. He said, "Okay." So, that's how I gave up my original name.

Later some friends and I put some money together to take the bus to Kakuma. I went there knowing my name had been used already. I said, "I need my name," but was told my name had gone already. A friend who had already left, told me to take his name, because it hadn't been used due to the mix-up when he signed up at a school. His name was Angelo, but the school administration had given him the name Arkangelo. He wanted to immigrate with the name Angelo, but the authorities gave him another name. So, Arkangelo was still available. He called me and said, "You better take my name." I told him I didn't want anybody else's name. He told me during citizenship I would have the right to change my name, so there was nothing wrong with me coming with that name. So, that's the way I became Arkangelo.

I applied for that name and received my immigration papers. And now that I live here in America all my American friends know me by Arkangelo, and even my Lost Boy friends know me by this name.

Becoming a refugee in the United States

I took my first flight from Nairobi to London. I spent five hours in London. When we took off from London again, we came to O'Hare International Airport. It was eight hours from Africa to U.K., and eight hours from U.K. to America. When we came to the airport, they took us to Homeland Security and gave us a work permit right away. I never had a passport or visa; we came through with immigration papers, as a refugee. We had to spend some days at the airport while we waited for Social Security to come through. I also had to take out a travel loan before even coming to America. I didn't have any money, so we made an agreement that I take out this travel loan and when we come to America we pay them back. The loan was from World Relief, a total of $852. They gave us three years to pay it back at $35 a month. But once I got a job they made me pay back more, I had to pay $100 a month. I was able to pay it off in a year or so.

I was welcomed by World Relief in Aurora, and they gave me an apartment. I spent two days not knowing my friends were here until a Sudanese World Relief caseworker told me there were some Sudanese here and some were Lost Boys. He told me to meet his friend Moses, who was also a Lost Boy. I used to live in an apartment alone in those days. For the first days I was there, I knew nobody. So, he told Moses, "One of your Lost Boys is here from Kakuma, and he is called Arkangelo." I said, "I don't know any Moses." In America, you call people by their first name and then last name, not by their nickname. When I talked to him on the phone, he gave me his name. He said, "I'm Moses." I had known him before, so I was very happy. He was surprised to hear I was here. He said, "When did you come here? How long?" I said, "Only two days ago." He said, "Oh, no, man, I can't imagine. Tomorrow I'm going to see you." On Sunday, we went to the Sudanese Community Center. My caseworker never had to take me home again. I was given rides home to my apartment from my friends. They came to Aurora to pick me up. That's the African way.

When I came here, I had a problem. Chicago is a big city with many suburbs, and I am from a rural area. The first thing I remember was that I had a problem with taking a shower. I told the caseworker that I wanted to take a shower and go to sleep. He told me to turn the dial and the water would come out. I removed my clothes and opened the shower, and the water didn't come on me. I stayed in the shower for five minutes waiting for the water. I put on my clothes again and went into the living room and told him the water was not coming out. He then explained how I had to pull a lever for the water to come out.

Then a week later, the police came to our apartment. I don't know why, but the police came. The police in Kenya used to wear light blue uniforms, but here, the police wear dark uniforms. So when they came in, I didn't know they were police. Maybe there was something going on in another apartment. Our apartment had a front door and a back door. They came in through the back door, so I went out of front door. I knew there were Somalian people who lived close by so I was trying to get to them. Maybe a description was given that resembled me or something. I don't know. So when I came out of the apartment, there were about four people calling for me, but I didn't know they were police, so I ran away from them. They said, "Why are you walking away?" But I didn't pay any attention to them. This was right by the public aid office and a lot of people were there, and they were staring at me. They let me go, and I went back to the apartment. After three weeks, a police car pulled up in the parking lot and that is when I realized that the people who were following me were policemen.

While I lived in Aurora, World Relief gave me a job, but I couldn't afford a car so I rode my bike back and forth from work. It was not easy during this time. It was very far away. I was working beyond Aurora in Montgomery. In the morning I had to ride the bike, but at night I walked back. It was really hard. I only worked this job for two to three months, but quit because of the snow. And then one of my American friends I met at the PRC gave me a car. That is a great gift I will never forget. They gave me a car without me paying anything. I started looking for a job and found one through an agency. I worked with the agency for three months and then was hired by the company.

In the beginning of 2007 I was working for a plastic company that produces parts for dishwashers. This factory was in Schaumburg. I worked there until November 2008 when the economy went bad and I got laid off. After I got laid off, I got another part-time job in Wheaton. I worked there from 2009 till 2012. I went back to Sudan twice, first in 2009 for two months, and when I came back they still kept the job for me, but then in 2010 and in 2011 I went again. After that, they said if I went back to Sudan I would lose the job, but I had to go back and see my family. So in 2012 I lost the job. Before I left in 2012, I got another job, and they said that when I came back, maybe they would still have a job for me. So when I came back and I got to keep that job.

World Relief gave me my apartment for three months. But when I met up with some Lost Boys who lived in Elgin, I moved in with them, and when I got a new job and had a donated car I learned how to drive.

My brother and my two sisters still live in South Sudan. My dad had a big family. He had two wives, so we have eleven people in our family. They are all alive; only my mom and dad are gone. My dad died of cholera. They were drinking water that was not safe for them. My mom died in a fire. Somebody set a fire, and she died with my older sister's two kids. My mom died in 1999, and my dad died in 1995. I was not aware of my father's death, but I came to learn of it when he was taken for treatment in Lokichokio. Someone came and found me in Kakuma and told me my dad had died. That was in 1997. That was the first time I heard from someone coming from my village. Somebody came from Sudan and told me what happened with my mom.

Life now is not bad, there are still some obstacles, but not like before when I had difficulty with English, and no transportation. I'm still living with some of my Lost Boys, and I managed to go back to Sudan four times now. I'm working in St. Charles at a factory. I make cables for electronics. I work three days a week and I go to school at COD [College of DuPage] for my GED.

In 2011, I became a U.S. citizen, but I also consider myself as a Sudanese citizen, although I have no paperwork to show for that. I was born Sudanese. I don't have paperwork, but I look like a Sudanese and I speak the language, so I'm always a Sudanese

The first two months I was here, I had a friend who played soccer, and he is the first one to take me to Chicago to see the city. I really enjoy Chicago. I did play soccer, but I retired from that now. I was pretty good back in Africa, but not anymore. We had competitions between the refugee camp and the local people in northern Kenya.

In 2011, South Sudan split from Sudan and became its own country. The outlook for South Sudan is uncertain. I want to help as much as I can in the rebuilding of South Sudan after the decades-long war. The Lost Boys, with the help of some Americans, have built a school, which is still in operation. Our plans were for a high school, but we did not have the funds. When I went home, I saw that there was no proper education for my nieces and cousins. I decided to put them in school in Kenya. There is no secondary school in South Sudan. The Lost Boys have plans for a secondary school, but we have not been able to raise the funds.

After we raised some money here, I went back to South Sudan to address one of the biggest problems in Sudan: access to clean water When my car was involved in an accident, the insurance company paid me for the car and I used part of the money to build a well, something that the people could use for a very long time, and part of it I sent to my nieces back in Sudan so that they could go to school in Kenya. A friend of mine, her husband, and friends then raised $12,000. I went back to Sudan to put in a well in my village, this was in 2011. A Syrian contractor and I became friends. He told me the more wells I could pay for, the more he would reduce the price for me. So in 2012, I was able to raise enough money for four wells, all in different villages.

I like Chicago and Illinois very much though. This place has become a part of me now, but I have a big problem with the snow and cold.

Though I am a U.S. citizen and enjoy life here, I also like to go back to my home country, especially when I can help the people there. South Sudan is where I'm from, and I will not forget that. My heart is still longing for South Sudan. That is my homeland, and I still have it in my mind.

❑

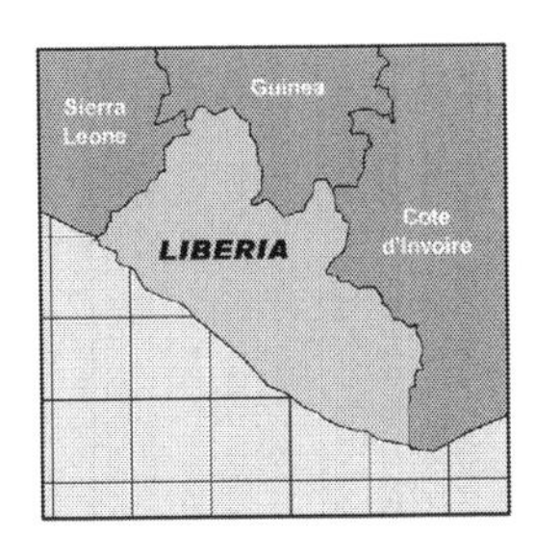

Raymond S.

Interviewed, 2008 and Spring 2014

I was born in Liberia, West Africa, in 1938. I grew up with my grandparents because my mother died when I was not yet two years old and my father left me and went to live in Monrovia, the capital of Liberia. As a child, I remember my town was warm and peaceful and we had a lot of trees. My grandfather was a farmer and no matter how much the people cleared the bush, the jungle would come back in six or seven years. While I was still a little boy, World War II started and my grandfather would tell us to go and hide whenever a plane flew over. My grandparents died when I was about twelve or thirteen years old. I then lived with my uncle for two or three years. Finally, my father came to get me and he put me in a mission school where I had my early education up to the eighth grade.

I started teaching, got married, and took a correspondence course from an American school in Chicago for my high school courses. I then went to a junior college, which was a teacher training school set up by the government for in-service teachers where I earned a teaching certificate. I taught for twenty-three years, from 1960 to 1983. In 1984, I moved to the city of Buchanan to do bible translation. Working with assistants, I translated the Old Testament into Bassa, one of the languages of Liberia. We worked with a computer and were helped by a consultant who had a Hebrew bible. I would translate into English and then check it against the Hebrew. We had done eight books when the war in Liberia started. When the rebels came, they destroyed everything. They took our books and piled them outside and set them ablaze, but they never touched the little box on the table with the disk which contained the first eight translated books.

Liberia used to be considered the haven of peace for the whole of Africa. When there was war, people would flee into Liberia for safety. When President William R. Tolbert was assassinated in 1980, all of a sudden things changed. In 1989, the rebels came into Buchanan and started shooting, and everybody was rushing into the streets to see what was happening. Many people were killed because they had no idea such a thing could happen in Liberia. Some of the rebels were as young as nine years old, they were drugged and they were given guns.

When the war got tough, people were leaving. Some of the neighbors were killed and their houses burned by the rebels. Nobody ever came to our house to hurt us. Life, of course, became much harder. Scarcity of food became severe and to continue the translation we had to move to Ivory Coast. We lived there from 1991 to 1998. By that time I finished the Old Testament. The New Testament was finished by the mission school I had attended.

The fighting finally died down and I moved my family back to Buchanan. I tried to do some renovation on our house which was still standing even though there were bullet holes in the roof. We were better off than the people whose houses were burned down. I was a pastor and when the rebel group came back, they did not like what I was preaching. They beat me severely and almost broke my right arm. They said they would come back and finish me. That's when my family forced me to leave. I easily got a tourist visa to the United States, but it took four years for my wife to get her visa. Five of our six children are still in Liberia. One of my daughters and her children live in DuPage County. We talk by cell phone to our children in Liberia.

The situation in Liberia seems to be improving. I am hoping to go back for a visit some day to see if it is possible to live there. Here, if I go to get a job, they look at my head...they would rather have a younger person.

When I first arrived in the United States, a Liberian friend let me stay with him. He got me a job with World Relief as a shuttle driver for refugees. I had that job for four and a half years. I got asylum through an agency in Chicago called the Human Rights Alliance. They did everything for free, including getting a lawyer. I will remain grateful to them.

When I think back I say, "No, I can't believe this happened in Liberia."

One of my sons works for the Lutheran Church training pastors in the villages. Another son is a technician in a Christian hospital, which also has a radio station. Jobs are still scarce in Liberia and for a man of my age jobs are scarce here in America. My faith is stronger because of what has happened to me. For instance, there is the story of my motorbike. I bought a bike in Liberia and had it for three months. Then, something told me to sell it. I did and the same week the rebels came and took everything from all the people. My family and I were able to live on the money from that motorbike for almost a year.

My faith is also strong because I have been helped when I came to this country. Between World Relief, St. Paul Lutheran Church in Wheaton, the Human Rights Alliance, and the People's Resource Center, I was able to get to this country and to get help to become a citizen. I have lived in peace and I have seen my own country torn apart by war, but I have the hope that I will go back to my country to live in peace again.

Editors' note: Raymond is a poet with poems in a PRC publication.

❑

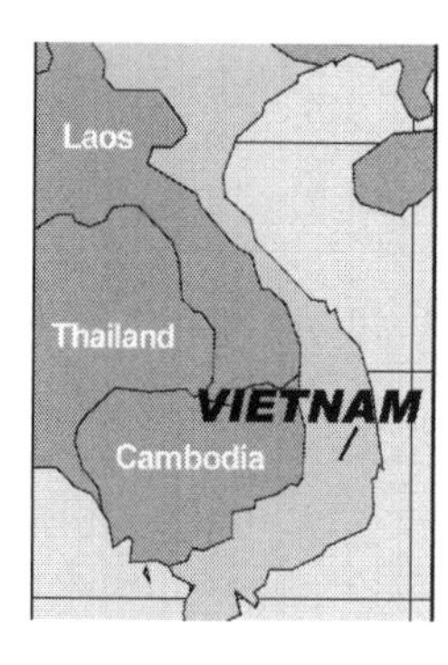

Leo B.

Interviewed, Spring 2014

I am fifty-seven years old and, like both my mother and father, I was born in Vietnam, Southeast Asia, in a small town of about five thousand inhabitants. I have one brother and one sister who both still live in Vietnam. My earliest memory is of my father and mother and a friend as we tended to the planting of the rice. I also remember the coffee and the tea. The highest level of formal education I had was elementary school, maybe fifth grade. The only job I had before coming to the United States was planting rice. I am married and have two children, a boy and a girl. I had three children, but my oldest boy died when he was twenty years old, before I came to America.

I have never lived anywhere else but Vietnam and here, in DuPage County. I was fifty-three when I left Vietnam. I was in jail in Vietnam for four years.

I like the freedom in the United States. I like the food in the United States. I like my life in the United States. I do not want to go back permanently, but I would like to see my father and sister again. My mother has passed away, but my father lives with my sister. I spent three years in Saigon before coming to the United States.

The biggest difficulties I had when I came to the United States were learning English, which I never spoke before, and dealing with the cold weather. It is very cold here, but I am used to it now. I also had difficulty learning to drive. But I go to church here and have friends there. I came to America with the help of the government and the World Relief organization. The World Relief organization helped me find the PRC.

The PRC helped me with food and to learn English. I also learn English at the church. I got a job last year, and English will help with the new job. My favorite thing about the PRC is learning English and having a job. I have told my friends about the PRC and how the people here are helping me. I am most proud of my country…this one.

❑

Martha S.

Interviewed, Spring 2014

I am from Sierra Leone, West Africa, and I do not know my age because I was born in a small village. My father had two wives. My mother had nine children and my father's other wife had four. My husband and I had six children, but two died in Africa.

Everything was peaceful in my village until the rebels came in 1991. They wanted to take over the land because they thought there were diamond deposits there. My family and I first hid in the bush and then fled to another part of Sierra Leone.

The rebels then came to the village to which I had fled. The other women and I were boiling palm oil that we used in cooking. Most of the women were able to run away, but my little daughter had just died and I could not leave her. The rebels were about to shoot me when one of them said, "Let's make her suffer." They then poured the boiling palm oil over my side and arm. The rebels then left me for dead and went away. I can remember that I was going in and out of consciousness, but I do not know how many days later it was when the other women came back. They found me alive, but very badly burned. They put me into a hammock made of twigs and sticks and carried me to the nearest town. There were no medical supplies or food in the town because of the rebel attacks. It was then I found that my husband had been killed by the rebels.

When the rebels came to this town, they captured my sister and demanded that she become the wife of one of them. When my sister refused, they shot her and left her body in the middle of the street. One of my other sisters is raising the children of my murdered sister along with her own.

The people then took me to the neighboring country of Guinea, but the hospital there did not have the medicines to treat my burns. Between Catholic Relief Services and the Red Cross, I was able to get to a hospital in Guinea where they could treat my wounds. But by this time, my arm was paralyzed and I was delirious. Slowly the treatments worked and the pain became less. I still have pain and my body is badly scarred and I have very little use of my arm. While in Guinea,

I lost another one of my children.

Through Catholic Relief Services, I was able to come to the United States as a refugee and my two daughters and my son came with me. My older son was already here. I think I was chosen because I was so badly burned and in constant pain. My sister, along with her children and our dead sister's children were not chosen and they now live in terrible poverty in Guinea. My children are now in high school here in DuPage County, but, unfortunately, they do not speak my native language any more. We speak to each other in Creole.

A friend from Sierra Leone brought me to the People's Resource Center where I started to learn English. I had been brought up speaking the language of my people and I did not learn English in Sierra Leone. I have never learned to read and write in any language. This is now a difficulty for me because I want to apply for U.S. citizenship, and I do not know enough English to pass the test. While studying English at the PRC, I joined an art class and some of my work is displayed on the wall of the art room.

I desperately want to help my sister's children to get out of Sierra Leone and come to the United States, but I cannot find anyone who is able to do this. I was told that the only way to help my family in Africa is to become a U.S. citizen and sponsor them. So that is what I am doing here at the People's Resource Center, learning to read and write English so that I can pass the citizenship test. I do not want anyone in my family to suffer the way I did.

> *Editors' note:* Martha is one of the most amazing women you will ever meet. The scars from her burns are horrific, and she winces often with pain. Because she is traumatized by the loss of her husband and children and her own torture and long journey to the United States, we interrupted the interview a few times, but she wanted to continue. She has found a way to ease her anguish by participating in the PRC's art programs. And with a tutor she is diligently working on her spoken English and learning how to read and write.

❑

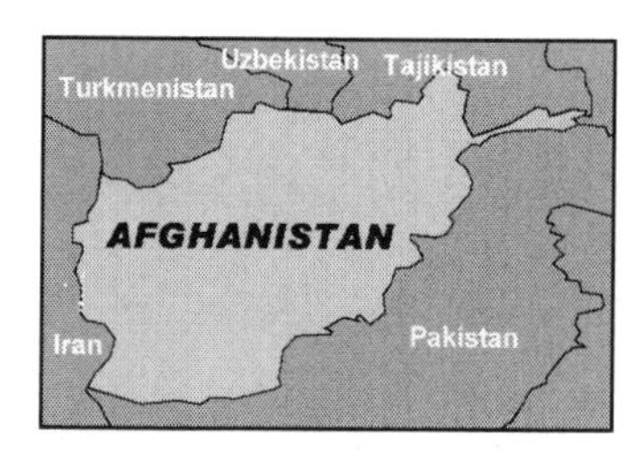

William Z.

Interviewed, Spring 2014

I am sixty-seven years old and, like my mother and father, I was born in Afghanistan — in a village of approximately 500 to 600 families. The only other place I lived before coming to America was Islamabad, Pakistan (for only two or three months), after I applied for a U.S. visa.

Growing up, I had four brothers and two sisters. All, except my older sister who has since passed away, still live in Afghanistan. As a child, my earliest memory was walking to school each day, and if I was late, the teacher would hit me. I did not have a bicycle and it was two hours both ways! My father was a poor tailor and so we also had no car, but that did not matter because there was no road.

I liked school. I went to elementary school, high school, and then two years of college to become a teacher, and I taught geography and history for many years. I had happy memories as a child, but after I had finished college, the Russians invaded in the late 1970s, and there was much fighting with the mujahedeen [the local fighters who battled the Soviet Union during their invasion from 1979 to 1989].The Russians tried to turn the country into a communist state and the mujahedeen, led by the village elders and tribal leaders, wanted to keep the traditional culture of the country. My eldest son was killed in the cross fire of the two opposing factions. He was not involved in any political or military activity, since he was a fifteen-year-old high school student. Life for me became also hard, because the fighting interrupted the teaching. Many times, the schools were closed, then reopened, then closed again. After the Russians withdrew, we had some quiet years, but then the Taliban made their appearance in 1996. By 2001, they reached our town and stopped people from going to school; it was very scary. The Taliban split from the mujahedeen forces and became very militant. The majority of the population in Afghanistan are Shiite Muslims, while the Taliban are Sunni who wanted to introduce a strict Sunni Islamic state — often with violent means. They tried to kick the Shiites out. I couldn't teach anymore, and it became unsafe, and in 2003 we decided to leave and apply to come to America.

My wife, my three daughters, and my surviving son, and I first fled our town by going up the mountain. After some time, my wife and two daughters decided to get to Pakistan. They walked many, many hours at night until they reached Peshawar on the Pakistani/Afghani border. They then crossed into Pakistan from where they immigrated into the USA. However, I didn't know where they were for over a year while I made my own way to Pakistan. I lost them for a whole year. Then suddenly a friend called and told me, "Don't worry, your wife and daughters are in the United States. Here is their number." My wife and daughters arrived before me, because they were sponsored by an American. So, I called her and she sponsored me, my son, and second daughter. She lived with two of my daughters and my son, my other daughter and I were assigned an apartment close by. We did not have enough money to rent a bigger apartment for all of us.

When I first came to the United States, the biggest difficulties I had were learning English and learning how to drive. But many friends helped me with transportation like driving us to church, but it was not always as easy as that.

I do not know if I am an immigrant or a refugee, but I do know that we had to leave Afghanistan. I miss certain things about home though. I miss the mountains and the river in springtime. But sometimes, I get scared at night and have bad dreams. My daughter has to wake me and remind me where we are. I do not want to go back home right now and I do not know if conditions have changed any — if they do, I may want to visit…one day.

I learned about the PRC through one of my daughters — she had a PRC card. At PRC, she studied English and they helped her to find a job. After that, my daughter became a psychologist, my son is an accountant, with an MBA, and the other daughters are in college. I study at PRC and at church, but my favorite thing about PRC is how friendly and helpful everyone is. They help with food, studying English, and learning the computer. I always try to tell people about the PRC and encourage them to utilize it.

I am most proud of learning how to drive a car and speak English. I am a College of DuPage student in a job class and my goal is to prove myself and keep learning. I would like to get a part-time job.

❑

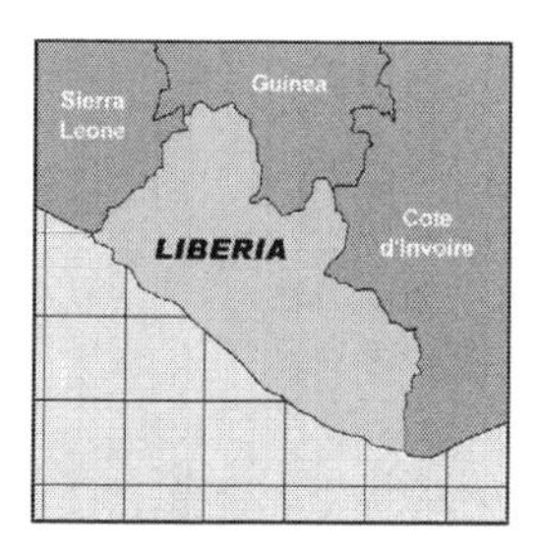

Julia R.

Interviewed, Spring 2014

I was born 1975 in Liberia, West Africa and grew up with my mother and father and one brother and two sisters, and I am the youngest child. We lived in a big town. I really loved living in Liberia, I mostly enjoyed living with my parents and neighbors, and you could do whatever you want there. We had no rules. The war started in 1989 and came to our area in 1999. I got married in Liberia but at age twenty-one I left Liberia. Eleven years later I arrived in the United States at age thirty-two.

My husband and I moved first to the Ivory Coast because of the war. I liked the Ivory Coast, it was a very good country. I lived in a small town with my husband and five children, who were born in the Ivory Coast. I now have six children, the last one born in the United States. I lived in a refugee camp in Ivory Coast that was run by the United Nations. It was bad and sad sometimes, no food to eat, we drank dirty water. I don't like telling people my stuff because it makes me sad. I lived in tents, my mother and father went back to Liberia because they said they would rather die in their own country than to die in the Ivory Coast in those conditions. The health conditions were really bad, I never went to the hospital, and I would pray to God that he will help me. My first five children were born in our tent, only my last one was born in the hospital, in the United States. There was a doctor in the refugee camps, but we would have to wait a long time for them to take care of us because there were thousands of us. People were dying sometimes with no food; the people watching us did not allow us to leave unless it was to buy something from the market. They monitored us all the time also, so we wouldn't spread the sickness that was happening inside the tents. They didn't allow us to work, only to brush and clean houses to make money.

We went back to Liberia; then the war started there again and we went back to the Ivory Coast; then in 2003 back to Liberia. We were registered to come to the United States. Liberia and Ivory Coast had people fighting, we had to stay in the bush and when we had to leave

Ivory Coast, we carried everything on our head and a child on my lap. I was running with my kids; my son got burned on his stomach, and I felt so bad about it. My mom and dad scattered around, I didn't see them before they died. My mother died in 2004 and my dad died in 2011. My brother died during the first war; we hadn't seen him since 1999. He died in the war and left his three kids and wife behind with nothing. The war is over, but we are still in it right now. My brother was my best friend, but I didn't see him before he died; his wife died a few years later and left the kids behind.

Search for relatives in the war-torn countries

I tried in 2007 to find my eldest sister; she went to college in the big city. I found someone to find her; I asked my husband for one hundred dollars to send to her; we found out she is in the bush with her children. She had been looking for our brother's children, and once she found them, she took them in. A short time later, her husband left her because she took care of my brother's children. I can't adopt them because they aren't my own children. She got mad at me because I don't take care of the children. They are all in Liberia. I don't have the money to send to them; she wouldn't believe me how the conditions are in the United States. My sister wants to leave the children because she doesn't have the money. I haven't seen my younger sister either. I only talked to her on the phone when my dad died. But right now she is sick. She had twelve children, three died; now she has nine. I want to go back, but there is no opportunity to. I want to see my two sisters and my brother's kids because they don't have a mom or dad, the oldest is sixteen, then fourteen and twelve. They don't go to school because no one can pay the fees for them to go.

Life in the United States

My husband has a job here. All my kids are going to school; my youngest child is seven. We had to register before coming to the United States, through World Relief. When we ran from Ivory Coast we registered in 2005 to go to America. They put is in a Fan C Compound; we stayed there for eight months before coming here. We went from Africa to France to New York then to Chicago. I didn't sleep because I was in fear. It took us a long time to get to the airport in Chicago. I was already worried. I didn't know anyone when I came here. A lot of my neighbors and friends came with me; there were about 300 people on the plane. When we came here we lived with a sponsor for one week, then we got an apartment. The apartment had two rooms and we had eight people to a room. The DuPage housing helped us and got us a bigger and better house. . My sponsors were so nice, but they moved so I no longer keep in touch with them. My church, St. Paul Lutheran, helped us out a lot. They also helped me find out about the People's Resource Center.

I couldn't read and write, but right now I am learning English and am taking an English course in the People's Resource Center. Liberia is English speaking, but I am trying to learn how to speak English better. My husband found a job, and I just started working. I work in a restaurant; I wash dishes in the kitchen. My husband didn't know how to read or write, but we both understand a little English. My primary language is Gedeh. I kept my dad's identification card, but I left everything else behind with me in Liberia. We came here with nothing.

Two of my kids are in high school and one is in middle school. They love going to school. They don't ever want to go to Africa because in the media they show Africa to be a horrible place when it is not like that all. This makes me very sad. I don't know many Liberians here because I stay with my kids at home when I am not working. My oldest kid is eighteen years old and a junior; he is very excited about going to college. The People's Resource Center gave me a computer in 2008 when I completed the computer course. My kids are usually using it. The people in Liberia are still struggling. There is no food and no opportunity for children to go to school. They don't have jobs so there is no income; it is still difficult for people. My family thinks I have so much money because I am living in America, but they don't understand that I can't afford to send money to them. I have bills to pay and six kids to support and feed.

> *Editors' Note:* Julia represents one of many interviewees who feel lucky that they were chosen to come to the United States. But they feel guilty that their close relatives who shared the hardships of war and extreme poverty were left behind. They feel guilty, despite the fact that they had no influence over the decision regarding who was selected. Their guilt and sadness is compounded by the fact that they cannot financially support their relatives who still live in poverty and under the threat of new wars or political upheavals.

❑

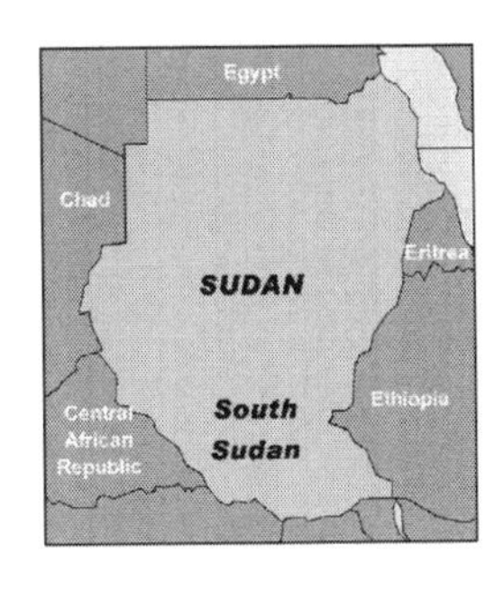

James P.

Interviewed, Spring 2014

I am forty-six years of age, and I was born in Sudan, East Africa. Sudan was still one country when I lived there. When I was growing up in Sudan, I had three brothers and only one sister. In Sudan, only some people were allowed to go to school, but for me I wasn't able to. Life is very difficult over there, most people have to work, and even in some areas there were no schools and to go it was very far, so I never did. I was born and grew up in North Sudan. I was born in Khartoum, but I moved to a village for a long time. My parents moved us, but went back to Khartoum when I was a big boy; the year was 1984. In Sudan I worked as a farmer, but later in the city I started working construction. When I lived in the village you work for yourself, but in Khartoum you worked for the government. When I was growing up it was very difficult. Everybody was looking for jobs. I never went to school; it was not good.

When I first went to Egypt I was thirty-three; the year was 2001. I left Sudan because of the war. It was a war between the government of Sudan and the rebels. I was not a "Lost Boy." The Lost Boys were only for the South Sudan people, but I am a Nuba Moro. But my three younger brothers were taken by the rebels for South Sudan. You know, the people fight for freedom, but they were taking young people. By 1987 the rebels were in the Nuba Mountain region and that's when they took my brothers. They were all put in a camp. One of my brothers escaped and is now back in our village, but neither he nor I know anything about the fate of our two other brothers. We haven't heard from them in at least four years. Nobody liked the government because it caused a lot of problems. Only a few people liked the government, they only helped a few people. They didn't give us clean water; Nuba Mountains didn't have schools. That's why we didn't like the government.

When I left, I went for Egypt in 2001; I was a refugee. Some people were allowed to work and I was one of them, so that made it possible for me to rent a place to stay and have a decent life. The experience in Egypt was good for me. I was working and rented an apartment. Even though I only made fifty dollars a month it was good for me. I got to stay in one place with my family. I had my wife and two kids. I didn't have anyone else with me though. I went back to Sudan in 2013. I went to Khartoum City. I couldn't go back to the Nuba Mountains because the government wouldn't let us go. There are still a lot of problems there. The government is everywhere. I only got to see two of my brothers. I didn't even get to see my father when I went back. I don't know when it will change with the government. I hope one day I can see my family, but I don't know when that will happen. It's been more than twenty years with this problem with the government, but the government is still making problems for us.

United States is a free country; everybody needs freedom, and if you don't have it, you look for it. In order for me to come here, I had to do interviews with Immigration. I had to tell the truth to them in order for them to let me and my family come. It took three years and two months for the immigration process to be completed. When we finally were able to come, we took a plane from Egypt to Germany, then from Germany to O'Hare Airport. Once we landed at O'Hare they took us to Fort Wayne, Indiana. The Catholic Church was helping us when we first landed, and they were the ones who took us to Fort Wayne. When I came to the United States on October 2004, it was hard finding a job. I was not a troublemaker when I came, just wanted to find work. It was winter, so dealing with the snow was scary. It was the first time I ever saw snow. After ten months in Indiana, I had a friend who lived in Glendale Heights so we moved there. My first job there was working in the hotel business. When I came to Glendale Heights, World Relief started helping us. They were the ones who found me a job and a place to stay. I heard about the People's Resource Center from a friend and I came to learn how to speak and read English and took classes for citizenship. I passed my citizenship test and am now a citizen. My wife is now also taking classes at the PRC.

I am very happy with coming to the United States. It's free and has helped me whenever I needed it. Everyone has been really nice to me and always treated me well.

❑

Victims of Discrimination

Most human beings know what discrimination is. Either they have experienced it themselves or they have observed it happening to others. The interviews in this segment were put together because they highlight the fact that discrimination takes many forms and happens in many parts of the world.

Discrimination can be racial, political, gender-based, or economic. Whether it is suffered by an African-American woman on the south side of Chicago or by a man from Burma or one from Iran, the person being discriminated against feels there is no legal or social recourse. The only choice is to escape, and the escape can be dangerous if it is from an oppressive regime.

Like most of the interviewees in this book, those who have experienced discrimination are ordinary people who wanted a chance to live in peace, earn a living, speak freely, and seek an education for their children. The discrimination they suffered disrupted those simple goals and desires and made them victims who felt they had to flee. Now, however, they no longer feel like victims because they are able to pursue their goals with the help of the People's Resource Center.

❑

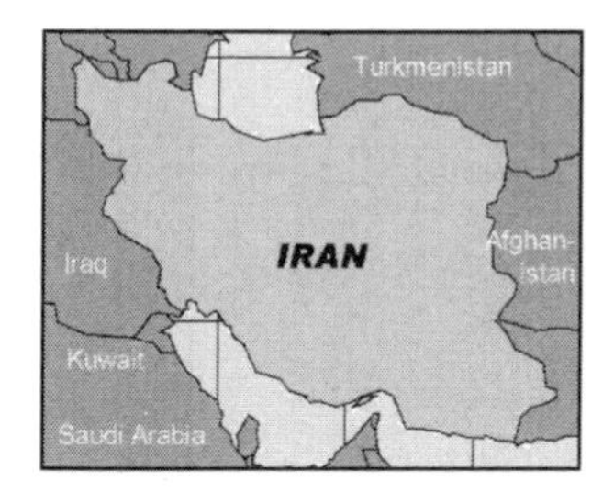

Mark C.

Interviewed, Spring 2014

I am fifty-four years old. I was born in Kurdistan, a region in the north of Iran, close to Iraq. I speak both Kurdish and Farsi. My three surviving brothers and one sister are still in Iran and one sister is in Europe. I received my high school diploma from Coresch High School and received my AA from Kurdistan College. After I finished school, I worked in a hospital for training for two years, but after that the government arrested me. When I was living in Iran, the government was very cruel to the Kurdish people. I and many others from my city joined the political party of Komalah. They stood for freedom and democracy. The government would not give us these rights. They would not help us in time of need. The government also would not help with the economy of our city. The government wouldn't help us with anything. One of the reasons they did not like us was because we had a different religious background. The government was made up of Shias and my city had many different religions. Also the official language of Iran was Farsi, while we spoke Kurdish. They were opposite of everything we were. I went to Jordan to speak to the United Nations about the mistreatment of our people, and after a month they arrested us and had us deported. The truly disappointing thing is that Iran is a very rich country, but they refuse to put the money into the people to make life better for us. Instead, they give the money to groups outside the country.

So because of the mistreatment we were receiving, there was a war going on between the people and the government. It was awful for us. The government was responding to the people by murdering us in cold blood, fifteen to thirty people a day. The way they would do this was to knock at your door and when you would answer they would put a bag over your head and take you away. They did this to me and my brother and five cousins. After several days of being locked away, they called me and told me they wanted me to go into the courtyard. As I walked there I saw a stage that had my brother on it. My brother had a noose around his neck. As I was staring at him, they kicked his feet out from under him.... They made me witness my brother's struggle till it was over. This still scars me today. I'll be driving down the road and see a stoplight, and the image of my brother appears on the stoplight.

After what they did to my brother I had to escape. After five attempts, I finally escaped from prison the first time and walked for a day to Iraq, where I stayed for ten years, working in a hospital. During this time, I quit the party, and got married to an Iraqi woman, and had one son. In Iraq, I was pretty safe, since I stayed in the northern part, which had a Kurdish majority. But then the Kurds and the Iraqi government under Hussein started to fight. I decided to go back to Iran. My wife, who was Iraqi, entered Iran with an Iraqi ID card, but a few miles before the border, I started walking around the border guards. Though I had an Iraqi ID card, I knew I was wanted by the Iranian police, since I had escaped ten years earlier. I met up with my wife in a hotel, but at 1 A.M. the Iranian secret police interrogated us for one hour. When they let me go, I went to my home city, but it was so changed after fifteen years that I took a cab to the wrong address. When I eventually found the right address, I knocked at the door, but my father wouldn't let me in, because he didn't recognize me. But my mother recognized my voice and they let me in. We all thought it was better, if my wife and I didn't stay at my parents' house, so we moved to another state to my brother's house. My father gave a friend whom he trusted my new address, but the friend betrayed him. Since I knew that if I visited anybody or they visited me, they would be subject to imprisonment, I stayed by myself and didn't talk to anybody. But one day, the house was swarmed by police and I was arrested and taken back to jail. My wife was also arrested and put in jail for fifteen days, but because she had an Iraqi passport with her maiden name, they let her go. She and my son stayed with my brother.

I stayed in jail for three years, and was tortured. I still have three bullets in my body. They always had me taking trash out to be thrown away, but every time I went outside, I would observe everything I saw. Where the guards stood, where they walked, which ways they walked. I made sure I knew everything about what was going on. This is how I was able to escape. When I finally did, I first went to Teheran to visit my best friend. He helped me to escape to Turkey. I left by myself and walked for a month till I reached the refugee camp in Turkey. The year was 1998. I stayed there for six years, but because I was a refugee I couldn't work. My wife joined me and we had another son.

I still have not been back to Iran.

While I was gone, my parents had a memorial service for me, thinking that I was dead, since nobody knew that I had escaped. At the service, everybody was arrested for a short time and questioned.

I came to the United States in 2003. It was not a pleasant experience. An international agency helped me get here and get situated. My English was not very good, and I couldn't read it. The agency people had me sign a lot of paper work, and I would ask for help on what I was signing; they would just tell me to sign and that it was ok. I did not like that. When I first got here they had me and my family stay with an American family for ten days. They kept us caged in one room the whole time. They would not help us get food; we were all very hungry and the American family was very difficult. I knew some British English and I would say, "food," "eat," "shopping," and they would say they couldn't understand me. It was obvious they just did not want to help. During the first month of my stay in the United States, there were problems with the agency that brought me. I had a Link Card for food and cash, but I was not able to use it as I needed. At one point, I told my caseworker that I did not want to stay in the United States any longer.

We had a third son in the United States.

I heard about the PRC and came for help. I have been working with a tutor and learning English at the PRC.

❑

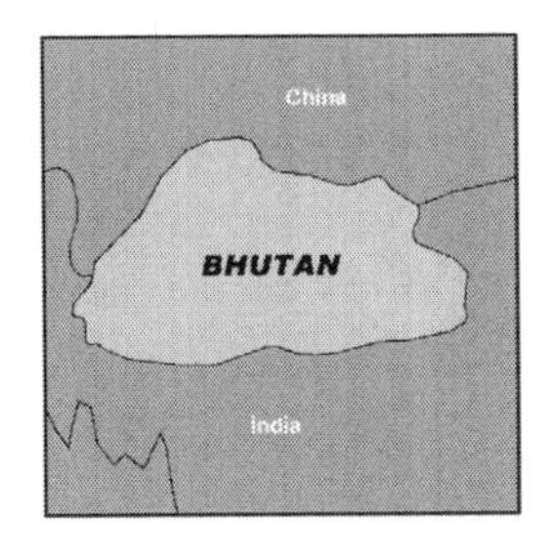

Danielle K.

Interviewed, Spring 2014

I was born in Bhutan, South Asia. When I was growing up, there were five of us children. There were two boys and three girls. I only stayed in Bhutan until I was seven years old. Then my family and I were forced to leave the country and move to a refugee camp in Nepal. In Nepal I was able to finish school to the eighth grade. When I was growing up, I do remember having a good life. I lived in the countryside in Bhutan. Our culture is defined by having a strong family relationship. We always lived together.

The story that my parents told me why we left Bhutan was because there was a fight between the government and the public. There was no freedom of speech, no democracy, and no human rights. The public wanted to have these rights. They felt that as people of Bhutan they deserved these things. But the government didn't like to give these rights. So there was a fight between the government and the public, but the government won and they kicked out the people. My parents also told me that Bhutan is a Buddhist country and that they speak Dzongkha. But my great-great-grandparents were from Nepal and they were not Buddhists. The Nepali people are known for their architecture, that's why the Bhutan government, many years ago, allowed fifty families from Nepal to come to Bhutan so they could work for Bhutan. But these people, including my ancestors, stayed after their work was done and started families in Bhutan, and this is why the Nepali-speaking Bhutanese community was increasing in numbers. The people who came from Nepal kept their family traditions, including language and culture, despite living in Bhutan. The Bhutan government started looking at the Nepali-speaking Bhutanese's growth and didn't like it, especially since we were Hindu instead of Buddhist. The government wanted us to act more Bhutanese; they wanted us to cut our hair and wear a uniform for school and the office. The government then did a census and wanted my parents to show our documents but my parents did not have the documents so we got kicked out of Bhutan.

Our journey was very sad. The government made my parents always carry citizenship documents around to show that they were citizens of Bhutan. One day my parents were walking around and the police made my parents show documentation that they were citizens, but when they handed them the documents, they took them and never gave back the documents. Then the police told my parents to smile and they took a picture of them. The government wanted these pictures so that they could show other countries that these people the government was kicking out wanted to leave. The government lied to us. It was very sad. We had to leave our home, neighbors, and friends, everything we knew we had to leave. The government did not allow our parents to bring anything but us children to Nepal. We left everything behind. As soon as we left, the government took everything, our cow, house, fields, everything. My parents still have not forgotten that day. We came with neighbors in a truck, which was very crowded.

I wish I could go back to Bhutan; I'm hoping after I receive U.S. citizenship that I can go back. I still have lots of family there: aunts, uncles, and my husband's sisters are all there. I want to see my land again. Although my family's house and land is all gone, I still want to see it. The government, after we left, divided up our property and built new homes and sold them to other people.

When we lived in the refugee camp in Nepal, it was a very tough life. In the beginning, so many people died because of illness. There were no good homes, food, or help. It was really bad. We had a very small tent and if it rained it went through the ceiling and onto us; if the wind blew hard our tent went with the wind. Eventually, we received help from different agencies and they provided food, shelter, and medicine. In time they would build schools for the children and hospitals for the sick. They even had police for the refugee camp. Having the schools built was very important to me because I wanted to learn. It was one of the happier moments for me in the refugee camp when I went to school and could learn. School is also where we made friends and got to act like kids again.

Our stay in the refugee camp was very long. We stayed there for twenty years. We did that because we wanted to go back to Bhutan, but the Bhutan government was not willing to take us back. We attempted to go back, and we did really try to move the government to take us back. We wrote letters to the government to let us come back, but our leader finally gave up and that's why we decided to come to the United States.

There were a lot of challenges I had when I came to the United States, but the most difficult was learning English. Before coming to the United States, I knew some British English, but the accent compared to U.S. English is different so I did not know very much when coming here. I learned more English here. Also everything is different in America from where I came from, so adjusting to that was difficult as well. Luckily I came with my husband, our daughter, and his parents to the United States. We are the first family out of our extended family that came to the United States, so I had to leave my parents, brothers and sisters, and all friends and relatives behind. It was really hard. But later, other families started to come to the United States.

The journey to come to the United States was very long and tiring. The flight was eighteen hours long from Nepal to Paris then New York then finally O'Hare Airport. I've never seen such a big place like O'Hare Airport. It was very scary when we arrived, because I have never experienced flying before this. Back in Nepal and Bhutan, we always took the bus everywhere we went. Flying was very new to me. When we got to O'Hare the World Relief Agency that brought us here told us to wait at the airport for someone to pick us up. But it seemed like nobody was coming; after a very long time we asked someone to help us. He told us where the baggage claim area was and that's when we found the agency that was there to pick us up. They were the ones to help us with all the paper work to get to the United States. Also they paid for our flights to come here, but it was like a loan because after we got to the United States and we found jobs, we had to make a monthly payment to them until our flight was paid off. The agency that helped us find jobs and an apartment was World Relief. We lived for four years in an apartment, and now we own a house. We bought the house from Habitat for Humanity. It's a very nice house and we like it. For finding jobs, World Relief first put us in English as a Second Language classes so we could speak English better. They also gave us a job class, which dealt with how to apply, interview, search for jobs, work with coworkers, anything and everything with jobs. It was very helpful for us.

World Relief was the one who helped us find the People's Resource Center. They told us that the PRC was the one that would help give us food, and they could give us clothes if we needed them and give classes to help with whatever we need. The best class was the computer class because they gave us basic knowledge of computers and at the end of the class they gave us a computer, which is very nice; I still have the computer that they gave us. I took some ESL classes at World Relief after that they told me that I could take higher-level classes so I went to College of DuPage for my ESL classes. The PRC is helping me with my GED classes, so that is what I am taking right now.

I do enjoy living in America; it's not Bhutan, but it is nice. I really like Christmas time, and I also like Thanksgiving. I really like American culture. I've been to downtown Chicago only four or five times, but when I go it makes me very happy. It's so beautiful there. It gives me a chance to see something different, people and buildings. The culture is different, but really good. Even Lake Michigan, it doesn't look like a lake, because it is so big, and it adds a good feeling to Chicago.

My background is Hindu. Religious freedom is not guaranteed in Bhutan, but these days many people follow Jesus. If I was in Bhutan or Nepal I would be looked down upon because over there following Jesus is not approved. In Bhutan we have a cast system and only the lower casts would follow Jesus. It is very bad for anyone who follows Jesus in Bhutan because people would not let you enter their house and they would not eat your food. I do like to follow Jesus though because when I was in the refugee camp my neighbors were believers of Jesus. My mother-in-law was very strict and did not approve, but when we came to United States we sat her down and told her that we need to follow Jesus because He is the way and the light for us. After a long time, my mother-in-law finally accepted Jesus, and at the same time we all went to get baptized together. It made me so happy when that happened. I am a Christian! We go to Agape Nepali Church in Wheaton every week, and my husband is actually a deacon for the church and he translates for the people because we have many Nepali people who attend our church. Also my husband is now the assistant pastor at our church. God has done so much in our lives and we are very grateful and happy for that.

❑

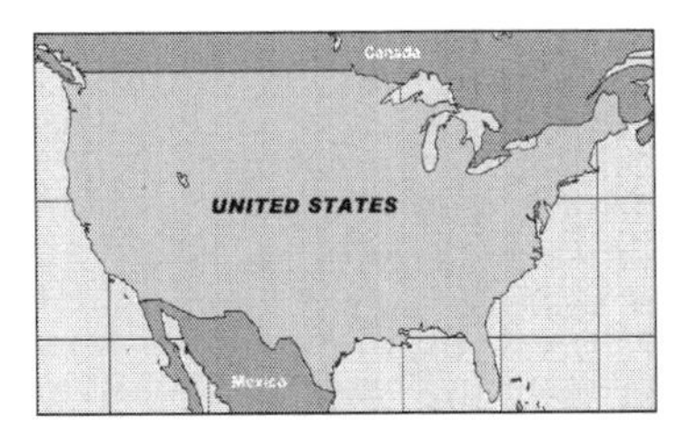

Susan N.

Interviewed, Spring 2014

I am a 71-year-old woman and a U.S. citizen. I have lived my entire life in Illinois and was raised in a small town south of Chicago. However, at the age of fourteen my family and I moved from our small town to the big city of Chicago. Living in the west side of Chicago was a much different experience than living in my hometown, due to the different density in each place. I had known almost everyone living within my hometown. That was not case in Chicago. I grew up as the oldest of fourteen children and helped my parents with my many brothers and sisters. At the age of eighteen, I moved out of my house to live in my own apartment. After moving out of my house, I had many different jobs, but of all the jobs that I had, the most memorable was when I worked as a Job Corp screener in which I interviewed teenagers for occupational training.

Living in Chicago was not only different in the fact that it was a larger city, but I also felt the pressure of segregation more strongly. In Chicago, I went to an all-black high school, and what I noticed during my years in high school was that segregation for black males was even more enforced than the segregation for black females. The police force also commonly messed with black males while they usually left the black females alone. Sadly, this type of behavior can still be seen in many parts of Chicago even decades later. During high school, I worked for Wesley Memorial Hospital in Chicago, and after graduating from high school, I worked several different jobs and acquired two years of college experience. I now have two daughters. One lives in a suburb of Chicago and has two daughters of her own, and my other daughter lives in Indiana and has two sons. I currently reside in a suburb.

I first came to the People's Resource Center, after hearing about the program from a friend whom I told that I had wanted to volunteer. I volunteered off-and-on at the food pantry for six years, but due to distance, I am not currently volunteering at the PRC. However, when I was volunteering at the PRC, I also took an art class for one or two sessions. Currently, I am working with the director of the Art Program to market the purses that I learned to make through the PRC. Another volunteer is helping me establish a website in order to market my purses to the public. Still another volunteer took pictures of my purses so that I could upload the pictures and sell my purses from the website Fran created.

Although I have only been making purses for a relatively short time, I have been sewing for a while now. After high school, I bought my first sewing machine in order to make my own clothes. I had always been very tall and thin, making it difficult to find clothes that fit correctly. I then took classes at a school for tailoring in Chicago to enhance my skills. When I came to the PRC for the first time was when I switched to making purses instead of clothes. When I took my art class, our class was making crafts. In order to be different and stand out, I chose to make purses due to my sewing skills while the rest of the class made jewelry to market.

Although I now live in a suburb, my family and I had some very exciting as well as very difficult experiences when we lived in Chicago. One of the most exciting experiences I had while living in Chicago was marching with Martin Luther King Jr. during the Civil Rights Movement. I marched with Martin Luther King several times including in Gage Park, an area known for segregation and white violence against black visitors. I had another experience in Gage Park when I was in my twenties, but it was not a good experience. One day when I was out working for the Job Corp, I stopped to eat my lunch in an unfamiliar park. I pulled a blanket from my car that I always carried with me and set up in the park to eat. However, all of a sudden when I began to eat I saw three young white men from a distance walking hastily toward me. In order to not cause a scene or draw attention to the fact that I was unnerved, I calmly packed up my lunch, acting if I was done eating, folded up my blanket, and walked to my car. The men still kept walking toward me, but luckily I reached my car before they could get a hold of me. However, I still heard their racist remarks as I made my exit.

After my incident in Gage Park, my uncle had an even more devastating experience while living in segregated Chicago. One day, coming home from work at night, my uncle was attacked by three white men. He was beaten up so badly that he was sent to the hospital. His injuries were so severe that he went blind from the attack. Sadly, my brothers suffered an even worse fate in 1971. Two of my brothers with their friend were murdered by the police while surrendering. My mother, clearly devastated by the event, spent all the money see could to get justice for my two brothers, but only one lawyer would pick up the case only to drop it soon after. However, even after all these events, I still remain positive that each person gets back what they give.

Although the Civil Rights Movement did produce many more rights for black males and females, racism and segregation still remain in Chicago and even in some of its suburbs. For example, every Tuesday I play cards at a senior center, and I am the only African-American. Although few senior center residents have made direct racist remarks toward me, I can still hear some of their sly remarks under the table. Also, the stereotype that black females will just submit to any male is still believed by many people in our present society. I had my own experiences with this stereotype, including one more recent event while I was working as a crossing guard before retiring. The same man every day would say "Hi" to me while I worked, and I, of course, would say "Hi" back. However, one day he invited me to visit him at his office. I did not think much of it, and decided to visit him. When I entered the building where his office was supposed to be I noticed that something was off. I did not want to assume the worst so I went to where his office was supposed to be. When I entered the door of his office he locked it behind me and began to make advances. However, I luckily was able to make an escape. I felt extremely disrespected and began to ignore the man when I would see him in the mornings. All in all, I hope this stereotype and many others attached to the black population will be erased, and the Chicago-land area will become an equal place.

❑

Family Considerations

"It is the children, it is the children, it is the children...."

This sentiment, often accompanied by tears, was expressed by so many of the interviewees. In almost all of the interviews in this book, the family of the interviewee is an important topic. In this segment, the stories revolve around family, family members left behind, and those who have come to the United States.

The American distinction between close relatives in the nuclear family and distant relatives in the extended family is not universal. For most of our interviewees, uncles and aunts, nieces and nephews and cousins are close relatives and when they or their children have not been able to come to the United States the responsibility weighs heavily on those who have made it here. This feeling is intensified when the immigrant or refugee knows that their family members are in harm's way from war, an oppressive government, or economic conditions. Those who are here are willing to do anything to get their family members out of danger or to get them financial help, but they are unable to reach across an ocean or a border. Those who have made their way to the United States often live in guilt because they are unable to help their distant family members. Some have gone so far as to study for their citizenship test, even if they came to the United States without knowing how to read or write, just so that they may sponsor some of their relatives who were left behind.

For those who are refugees, the situation has been made worse because they may have been separated from their families, even from their children, while getting to a refugee camp. But, even if they were not separated in the camp, they have experienced the anguish of being chosen to come to the United States while other family members, especially adult children, were not chosen. The choices made by governments accepting refugees seem arbitrary and when a family is broken up the effect can be heartbreaking.

Those who reach the United States and can find jobs face an additional problem. If they are in touch with their family members in their home country, those family members consider them rich and expect some form of help. The fact that the refugee or immigrant is barely making a living wage does not make a difference. "If you are in the United States, you must be rich" is the message that comes by phone or text message from the home country.

Finally, there is the situation faced by those who have been in the United States for some time. Their children may have been born here or have spent most of their young lives here and they do not have the same feelings for relatives they have never met, for a language they have not learned well, or for a country they have never seen. Their attitude toward helping their "foreign" uncles and aunts or cousins is very different from that of their parents. They consider themselves American and their connection with their relatives in another country is the American attitude toward "distant relatives."

Many of the people we interviewed and put into the category of "Victims of War" also belong in this category, especially Martha S. and Julia R. They feel responsibility for the members of their extended families that they had to leave behind — and they feel guilty even though they had no influence over who was chosen to come to the United States. We put them in the War category because they have also experienced terrific hardships due to war during their journey to the United States.

❑

Monica F.

Interviewed, 2008

I was born in the 1930s in Costa Rica. My parents had seven children. My grandmother was wealthy, and she stored golden coins in big, empty tins of lard. That was the way they saved their money, because they did not have any banks at that time. My grandmother was very dedicated to the cattle that they had.

My father was living in a city. His family was all living there. The family was wealthy, but my dad was very poor. My father's brothers were wealthy, but they spent all of the money. Even after my dad got married, he and his brothers used to drink a lot and had girlfriends. They were not very careful and were disrespectful to my mom. When my dad's mother got very, very sick, my uncles transferred all of the property of my grandmother to themselves and basically left my mom and dad on the streets.

My mom raised us in total poverty. My uncles sent my mom and all of the children away to a very beautiful ranch to take care of the ranch. My mom had to work very, very hard just like any other employee. It was demeaning. My mom had many sorrows. *La cuarentena* refers to the forty days after delivery. She had to carry heavy sacks of products after she delivered me. The reason why my mom had to work was because my dad was never there. My mom's intention was to have me baptized, but there was not a chance until a German priest came and baptized me under a mango tree.

As I said, my grandma was very, very wealthy. She sent my dad to San Jose to study law. He almost became a lawyer, but his lifestyle ruined his chances of ever becoming a lawyer. My dad got involved in politics in the late forties when there was big political upheaval in Costa Rica. My dad got into politics again very deeply. Between politics and women, my father was barely home, so my mom had to work very, very hard. Just like they say, "like a mule." We used to be hungry all the time. My mother used to wash clothes for other people, and she used to iron their clothes. We, as little children, helped her clean the patios or courtyards and wash them off. We never stopped going to school. She always wanted us to go to school and get an education. The worst part of all was at nighttime, when we used to get sick, because the only thing we had to eat was beans. My brother had a good sense of humor, and he would count the beans he ate. My mom used to cry, and say please don't do that, because she knew it was very little. It would hurt her to know that he had to count them knowing that it was little. He was always in a good mood.

We suffered incredible poverty, but we did have happy moments in the midst of this. It was a very healthy childhood where we didn't have to worry about external things, like war. My mother would allow us to be on our own to go play, and we used to spend our time playing sometimes. We used to play jump rope and hop scotch. For Christmas, we never received anything. We could hear how happy the other kids were with their horns and their dolls. My mom used to bring us inside the house, so we would not feel sorry for ourselves or suffer. There was a very nice project through the school that dedicated themselves to make soup for all of the children. That's where we sometimes got more food. I used to help the janitor lady clean. I would beg for her to give me a bone with some meat and that's how I would eat sometimes.

Life was so hard, and there was a situation in which I was sexually abused. Life was very, very hard, because there was a gentleman who used the excuse of, "I will feed them, but I need them to help me with this." He looked at me in a different way. Then on one occasion, he touched me all over, and tried to sexually abuse me and my sister. But I defended myself, and I left the place running and crying. When his wife came outside to see what was going on, he lied and only said, "I was trying to reprimand her. Look at her, she's just crying, because I reprimanded her." I remember this all the time. One time, after I was already married, we ran into this man, and I introduced my husband to him. When we turned our backs to leave, he caught me from behind, gave me a hug and said, "Oh…," but my husband was a little further ahead of me.

After the president of Costa Rica was overthrown by the guerrillas, my dad became a political refugee. He would hide and run away, and that's when we would see him. He would come home to hide. When he would come, he was always angry. When I would see him, I would run and hide under the bed. Also, my brother and sisters would run and hide. My dad had another woman. There was an occasion in which my dad came. He was very angry. He hit my mom and left. After he left, my mom picked up a blade. In the past, they used blades for shaving. She picked up a blade and went into the bathroom, and she tried to commit suicide. I was outside the bathroom, begging my mom not to do it. That's what hurts me the most. That was the hardest. There was a second time in which my dad came and hit her again. My mom left and one of my sisters followed her. Her intention was to jump off a very high bridge. My sister saved her, because my sister held her, and said, "Mom, please don't do this, because then we will be left alone." You know, that was a very, very horrible impact. Now that I am older, I get very depressed. I get horrible depressions.

My father went to prison many times. They searched for him and imprisoned him. But that was his cure. After he was imprisoned, and when he was released, he would come home and work very, very hard. Once he was a little more stable, and he had a little bit of a better life, they would come and imprison him again. Once they told him that they were going to kill him. They put him against a wall, and gave him a cigarette to smoke: his last cigarette. They kept threatening him and saying they were going to kill him by shooting him, but they never did. It was just a way of torturing him. It was like three times that they did that to him. I think that that type of impact was what made him change totally, because he was an educated man. There was an occasion in which he and some of the friends were walking on the street. There were some snipers surrounding the area. It was just out of luck that he said he needed to do something else. He went across the street. His friends all kept walking down the street, and they were all killed.

After a while things were a little calmer, but they used to call my father a communist. It was a very, very hard word to use against somebody at that time, because if you were known as a communist, no one would give you a job. Because of the lack of work, he became a craftsman. He really dedicated himself to the job. He changed totally. He would say to us that he would take care of us, and he did after that. I was twelve years old then. My sister was working at a company. When her boss learned that my dad used to be called a communist, he fired her. We all became very close and helped in my father's business. My older sister only completed the fifth grade. The rest of us continued to go to school, but because she was the oldest, she dedicated herself to working and earning money. That's why she stopped going to school, but the situation got better for all of us. After a time, my dad said to her that she needed to go back to school. He said he would train her so that she would recover all the years she lost at school. He helped her a lot. She and two of my other sisters became professionals.

My dad was always very interested in us being good people, that we would have a good marriage, and that we wouldn't make mistakes. Everything was going very, very well. It was going so well that he thought that he was going to buy a property for building a house. At that point, we were still renting a place. He was going back to farming. He was going to harvest small trees called "mangle trees" that grow on the coast. At harvest time, they peel the skin off the tree, and they use that for extracting color to color leather. It was a very long process. He used to go on boats with employees to a place further into the water, and he would pick up all of the mangles and bring it back to the shore.

My dad used to take my brother with him, because he was old enough to start working. In the last trip, the boat turned over, and my dad and three other people died. My brother survived, but he saw my dad die. What saved most of the others was that there was a boat not far from them that was anchored. As soon as the man who owned that boat saw what had happened to our boat, he came to the rescue. My dad was only in his forties. After that, life was difficult again, but we became very, very close. We learned that we needed to become a close family. That's how we overcame everything. My brother and I were both married, shortly before my dad died. He used to love me. He loved me very much.

We continued to work very, very hard until my older sister decided that she wanted to come to the United States. In the 1960s, the American Embassy was recruiting laborers. If you had certification or some kind of a title that certified that you were qualified, they would recruit you and bring you to the United States. My husband was a skilled draftsman. That's how he applied, and we came to the United States. My husband came first, and then my daughter, son, and I waited there for a long time for the embassy to process our application. Then we received a residency permit, as did my sisters and my mom. Living here was hard. It was very, very hard at the beginning, but little by little, we were able to rise. And lately, thanks to God, everything is going very well. All of my sisters retired back to Costa Rica. My mom died at the age of ninety-four due to Alzheimer's and cancer. We used to live in the East, where I worked. When my daughter's family moved to Chicago, I followed them to be close to my granddaughter. I love Chicago. Only the winter is terrible. It's hard for us. I visit my family sometimes in Costa Rica, but I would not move back to Costa Rica.

> *Editors' note:* Monica was a client of the Adult Learning and Literacy Program at PRC. She was interviewed in 2008 by the interns at PRC under the supervision of Rosie Dixon. The PRC has lost contact with her, but she had given permission to publish her story then.

❑

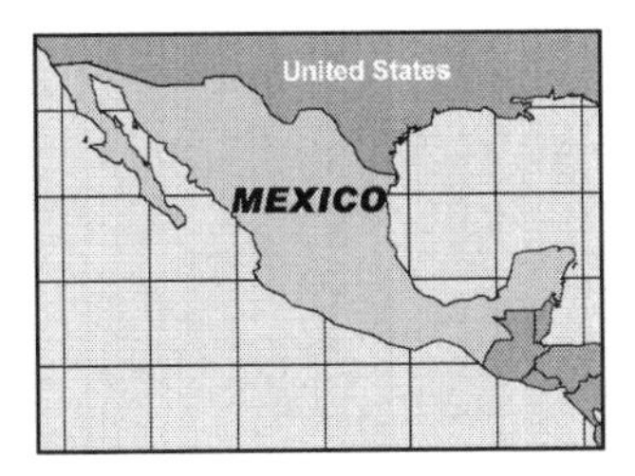

Vanessa M.

Interviewed, Spring 2014

I am in my forties. I was born in Mexico. Growing up there were eight children, four boys and four girls. Education in Mexico is different from the United States. I studied only three years in the elementary school, but in this country I have studied English for eight years. I studied for only three years because of where we lived. We had one classroom for all the people who lived in that area. To get a teacher to come to us, the teachers needed to walk an hour to get there. Sometimes the teacher came to class and other times they didn't. I was interested in school, but I didn't have a chance to go. We would walk to school five days a week, but the teacher may only show up two maybe three times a week.

As a child I worked to help my dad with the farm, feeding animals and tending to the crops. Growing up I was very happy living in Mexico. Sometimes, I talk to my children and I tell them about my childhood. I tell them how I didn't have all the things they have. Sometimes food was hard to get. My parents did not have much money or a lot of food, unlike in the United States. It was harder to survive in Mexico than it is here. We survived by my parents growing corn and beans. My dad had some cows to give us milk, and my mom had some chickens to give us eggs. My parents were farmers but they did not own a farm, they did not have very much, just enough to have the necessities to survive.

When I left Mexico I was twenty-six years old. I left Mexico because my husband had lived in the United States before I did and we dated for two years and he wanted to come back to the United States. This country gave us a better opportunity to live than Mexico. It's easier to get a job and make money. We married in Mexico then came to the United States. My husband also didn't have an education, so since we came here, he has worked in landscaping.

My journey to the United States was very difficult. I came illegally. I came through Tijuana and went to Los Angeles. I was able to come through the border because I used a coyote. Coyotes are those who bring people illegally. They charge us to come in the United

States. My husband had to pay $1,500 to the coyote. It was only for me. When my husband first came to the United States, he came illegally, but after he became a resident he was able to go back to Mexico and reenter the United States legally. The experience with the coyote was very difficult and dangerous, and I do not remember all the details. I traveled by bus from the closest town from the place I lived in Mexico to a place where there was an airport. From then on, I don't remember where we went, but I and about thirty other people were put in a house for two or three days. I just remember that the coyote got us from an airport and took us to this house. It was an unoccupied house. The house was very crowded; we had to sit around the rooms because it was full of people. They gave us one sandwich for three days and coffee in the morning. We never slept because everyone needed to sit with our knees to our chest just to make room for everyone to sit. While we were there, he made us an identification card, one for everyone, and then he put us in a big van and took us to another airport, I don't know where, and then we flew to Illinois. The flight was very strange; I don't remember the process about getting us in. The coyote did everything illegally. The coyote would not tell us much about what we were doing. When flying into Illinois, we flew on a commercial plane. We had other people on the plane besides just the people coming illegally. I never understood how the flight attendants didn't say anything about us. We were all in dirty clothes. We had to walk three hours before getting to the airport. Thirty people all in dirty clothes, and I would think that the people who were working wouldn't let us on, but they did. When I arrived in Illinois, we landed at O'Hare Airport. When we arrived my husband was there to pick me up. He had lived the whole time in DuPage County.

I am now a citizen of the United States so I am able to visit Mexico with no problems. The area where I used to live in Mexico has changed economically. My family lives better now than we did when I was there. My siblings have all grown up, so there are fewer mouths to feed.

Coming to the United States was very hard. My English was very bad, and this is the reason I wanted to learn it so bad. I would go to the doctor and I would have to fill out a medical history form, and I would have no idea what it said. I had to ask for help to fill it out; some people were nice, but other times people would not have the patience to help me. It was very hard. English was really hard because I didn't speak any at first. If I needed to go to the store, I couldn't ask for anything. One thing that was nice was before my husband and I got married, he lived with two of his sisters. They both got their residence permits in the United States at the same time as my husband. But they both came illegally like I did. After he came, there was a reform for immigrants that gave residence status to those who did not break the law. There was amnesty for immigrants; my husband got residence twenty-five years ago.

Finding work was not very hard for my husband when he got to the United States. My husband's first job was as a busboy at a restaurant. It was not difficult for him to get work. The boys from my area in Mexico who came to the United States wanted to work, so they worked very hard, and it didn't matter to them which job that they were able to get. I never had to work in the United States. I have two children, but didn't want too many; it would be too hard to care for many children. When it came to buying a house my husband and his brother bought the house, they had to buy the house together because he did not have enough income to buy it by himself.

When I came to the United States, I wanted to learn English so I went to register at C.O.D. [College of DuPage] in order to learn English. But the classes they had didn't work for me because I had to take care of my son and I also didn't drive yet. So the people at C.O.D. sent me to the PRC; it was the only place that worked for me. Since that day I still come to PRC to study English. Since I don't have an educational background, it has been really hard for me. Studying for my citizenship test, took me about nine years.

❑

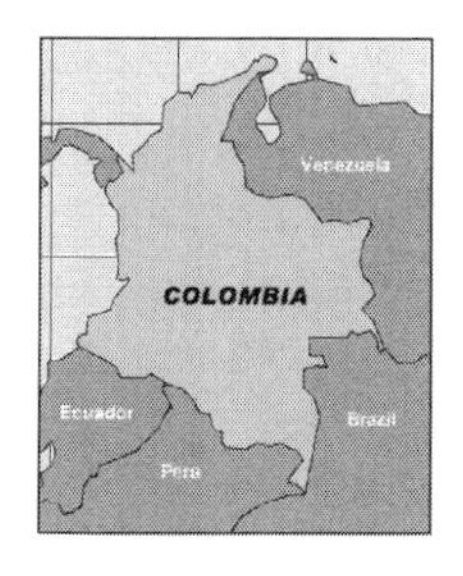

John G.

Interviewed , Spring 2014

I am 65-year-old male from Cartagena, Colombia, a port city in northwest Colombia. Not only was the city that I grew up in a prominent city in the region as well as the country, boasting almost a million inhabitants, it is also a very historic city. Founded in the early 1500s with the colonization of Colombia by the Spanish, Cartagena has a very interesting and important history. When the Spanish came into South America, many conquistadors and other Spanish immigrants and explorers came through the city of Cartagena named after another city in Spain. Through this city, the Spanish culture was able to expand and flourish, and the city was a center of political and economic activity due to the affluence of the city and the royalty. It was through this city that the Spanish were able to gather the South American gold that made the city so affluent. The city is also associated with piracy that occurred in the region and the large fortress that is a Unesco World Heritage Site. The large fortress that used to be a very important part of the Spanish empire in the Americas is now part of the busy downtown.

The historical significance of the city played a very important part in my life as well as in the life of my six sisters and brother. My father worked for an American company almost all of his life, allowing him to learn English very well, but he also worked as a tour guide in the city. I used to love to ride along with my father on his tours, where I learned more about the history of my city. Through my father, I also learned more about the American culture. Some of the people my father worked with, as well as some of our family's friends, brought us American goods as well as American customs. Among these friends were our neighbors in Colombia. The father was from the United States and came down to mine minerals, and the mother was from Colombia. I really enjoyed how close our families were, and it felt as if they were part of our family growing up.

From this family, my father's coworkers, and other friends of my father, our family was able to experience the painting of eggs on

Easter, which is popular in the United States, and we were able listen to American music, such as music from Broadway. Although we had many American goods and customs, I was not as interested in learning English as an adolescent. I just learned English in school in order to pass my tests. It was not until later in my life that I tried to learn English more intensely. I went to an American Center in Colombia where I took five English courses. Later when I came to the United States, I used to walk around with a Walkman trying to understand the language since Americans spoke English so rapidly.

My oldest sister was the first to come to the United States in 1970. She came without papers and documentation, but eventually became a citizen years later. It was easy for her to become a citizen, unlike now, due to the fact that immigration laws were not as strict. However, years later when I came to the United States, that was not the case. Unlike my sister, I had never dreamed or had any desire to move to the United States. In 1986, I married my wife in Colombia, and our family was in a good economic position so I never thought that I would need to come to the United States for work. I had a stable job and could support my family with the job that I had. However, the year that I got married, I asked my sister to claim me in the United States so that if something did ever happen, which I never thought it would, I would be able to enter the United States and find a job.

Even though I had asked my sister to claim me in 1986, it took ten years for all the documentation to go through allowing me to enter the United States. By 1996, our economic position had changed. I now only had a part-time job as well as two children and a wife. I could not support my family in the same way that I could ten years ago and felt that the only solution to our family's problem was to journey to the United States to make money. However, in order to do so, I had to leave my wife and my daughter, who was eight, and my son, who was three. Our family also had to sell our three-bedroom apartment, which took two years to sell, in order to come to the United States in the year 1997. Also, in order to come into the United States, I had to go to the embassy in Colombia to interview for a visa. However, I did not have enough money to venture to the embassy, which was an hour plane ride away, and pay for the visa. My uncle, thankfully, said that he would loan me money in order to come to the United States and get my alien visa, which meant that I could not bring my family. I said that I would pay him back once I got to the United States and started making money.

When I first came to the United States at the age of forty-eight, I lived with my sister for a month and a half. I did not particularly like living with her and looked for other living arrangements. I found another place to live when a friend of my mother from Argentina and her husband from Yugoslavia said that they had a room in their house that I could rent. They also said that when I started making money I could pay them back, and I lived with them for three years. Eventually, I did find a job in the United States at a nursing home, but in 1999, I visited my family in Colombia. When I went and visited my family, they said that I had to come and visit them for Christmas, but the nursing home would not let me take any days off in December in order to visit my family. Since my family always came first and still does, I quit my job at the nursing home and went back to Colombia to visit my family at Christmas.

I did not have a job for several months, and I moved in with some friends for four months. Eventually, I was able to get a new job at a company that tested soil as well as other substances. At the same time, I was assisting at a center in Naperville, which promoted the practice of being a vegetarian, which I eventually became. I met a friend there who said that he found a room for me that I could rent since I wanted to move. This friend also helped me find another job closer to the new room in Naperville since I was commuting a long distance to my other job at the testing company. The new job was at an Indian dress company where they made very fancy dresses for special occasions, and the pay was the same as my other job. However, six month later, the people at the testing plant where I had recently quit started to unionize, and the pay went up to seventeen dollars, making me regret leaving the job.

During the time that I worked for the dress shop, about four to four and a half years, I was asked by the Indian owner if I wanted to stay in his multimillion dollar mansion. He asked me if I could nanny his children as well as work at the dress shop, and if I did a good job as the nanny-of-sorts for the first three months, he would pay me extra money. However, after three months of me working hard, he said that he did not have the money to pay me. Since I did not want to be treated as a slave, I decided that I would ask to leave the babysitting job and still try to retain my job even though while working at the shop I had gotten a lesion in my knee from grabbing the boxes from high shelves. My job at the company was in shipping and packing, which caused me to have some physical problems. Eventually, six years later, I would have to get surgery in my knee to fix my meniscus.

In 2000, I finally acquired enough money to move my family to the United States, which meant starting to do the paper work to bring them. However, I could not move them until I became a citizen in 2004 due to the fact that one of my sister's affidavits of support would not be accepted by the government. I provided my family with $6,000 to try to come to the United States, which was supposed to cover their ticket to the embassy to get their visas as well as the hotel to stay in the city where the embassy is located. However, my family was not able to come to the United States right away, and all the money went to waste. I then went to seek answers for why my family could not come and what happened to the applications. When I went to ask someone in government where the application had gone, he said that he would tell me what happened to it for twenty-five dollars. When I did give him the money, he told me where I could ask someone else about the information, which was a complete waste of the money. I ended up going to talk to a congresswoman of Illinois who helped me get the visas and the permits to get the children and my wife to the United States. I was worried that I would not be able to get my daughter to the United State in time because she would be turning eighteen soon. When she would turn eighteen, she would be considered an adult and not able to come and live with us. Thankfully, I was able to get her and the rest of my family to the United States by 2006 only a few months before my daughter's birthday.

Currently, both of my children are U.S. citizens. My daughter is in her second year of college, studying nursing, and my son is in his first year of college, studying to become an engineer. Both of my children are studying at the College of DuPage and have part-time jobs. My wife was not able to become a U.S. citizen until last year. A great majority of my nieces and nephews also reside in the United States and are citizens. One of my nephews is an engineer for the company Caterpillar in Peoria, Illinois, and another is a sanitary engineer in either Champaign or Springfield. He got his first job at the testing company where I had once worked; I was the one that had told him about the job. One of my nieces also lives in the United States and graduated from DePaul with a psychology degree, while another one of my nieces also graduated from college with a degree in graphic design. I also have another niece who is an architect in Florida. As for my sisters, I have a sister who is an accountant, another who lives close to Wisconsin and is a teaching assistant, and another, the youngest sister, who works for an unemployment office. One of my sisters still lives in Colombia with her husband and is doing well.

Now to go back to my education and job experience in Colombia, I graduated from high school with a diploma and went to a Colombian university for a year to study architecture. However, I became very interested in a young lady and lost focus causing me to not do too well in school. The university would not let me continue in my program, and I began to study economics for a semester although I learned I did not like it fairly quickly. I then moved on to study business administration, but at the same time, I was working for a construction company in which I was making good money. I decided to leave school since I did not think I would need a degree, and I kept that job for ten years in which I worked with contracts for the company. I then worked for a government company for six years in which I was a paymaster and treasurer.

Of everything that has occurred in my life, especially in the United States, one of the biggest difficulties that I faced was the struggle between the U.S. Embassy in Colombia and my sister's affidavit of support, which the office refused to accept in 2001. I had to wait another six years to bring my family to the United States to live with me. Several times when I would go to the mall I would see a family walking, and the children I would see in the family would be the same ages as my children. I would have horrible pains in my soul since by coming to this country, I had to say goodbye to my family. What was also a very difficult situation was when my wife had her breast surgery, and I had to work two full-time jobs in order to have enough income to support my family and her surgery. I also had a lot of problems with the English language. I suffered a lot since I had to start work in the United States knowing very little English.

When my family first came to the United States in 2006, I came to the People's Resource Center in order to get food and clothes for my family. We had to go to the center for several years until I could obtain a better job. I have also taken computer classes in their programs. I appreciated and still appreciate all that the PRC did for my family, and I feel that only God can truly pay them back for their goodness. In the end, after all of my experiences, I had to accept the life God gave me, and I found it very helpful for me to read a book by Brian Weiss, head of psychiatry at a hospital in Florida.

❑

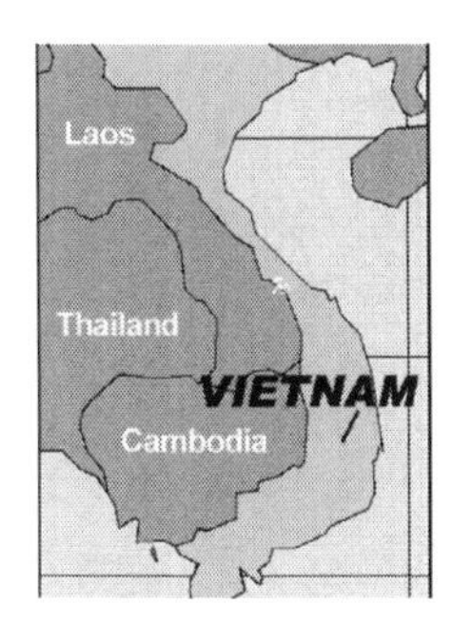

Lucy B.

Interviewed, Spring 2014

Editors' note: This interview is basically a comparison between life in Vietnam and the Unites States.

I am twenty-two years old. I live in DuPage County. I was born in Vietnam, and lived only in Vietnam. I have an older sister and a younger brother. I went to high school in Vietnam. Right now I am not going to school, but I am looking for a school to attend. I work at a beauty store, and I volunteer as a cleaner. I want to do the physician's assistant program at College of DuPage. I am a medical assistant in the United States. I need some experience to get another job. I came here five years ago, my grandma, mom, and family wanted to move here so we all decided to come to the United States.

My life in Vietnam was really good. My grandfather was part of the army. In Vietnam I went to school where you spoke your own language; it was easier. I still talk to my friends in Vietnam. I talk to them about driving, which I don't like doing. My childhood growing up was good, and I get along with my family very well. I lived in a small village in the countryside. Right now, I really want to go back to Vietnam. My favorite thing was, when I was there, I liked to go to the farms and take care of cows and ride my bike to see the sunset. The living conditions were generally harsh, because it was often cold. My parents were farmers in Vietnam. My mom was never home so I had to take care of everyone and the house. My father worked very hard, he would ride a bicycle to the farm and back. Right now my father is working at a company and my mother babysits. My brother is at the College of DuPage, studying to be a producer. The most difficult thing I faced coming here was the language barrier. I didn't know how to speak English or even drive. This made it very difficult to find a job. My grandma helped us a lot; we lived with her. I was sixteen years old when I came; I miss Vietnam a lot. My sister also comes here to the PRC to speak better English. I like learning how to draw and to sew. We saved money and looked for a house; we pay for the rent all of us together. When still in Vietnam, I went to school on a bike. It was sixteen kilometers [about ten miles] back and forth. I had to wake up at four in the morning to get to school on time. The food in Vietnam is much better than the food here. The food here comes in large amounts. My favorite type of food here is a hamburger. We usually cook homemade meals. I'm not very good at cooking, but my mom is really good. I haven't made any friends because I can't speak good English. I want to make friends; that's why I want to speak better English. My brother speaks English very well; he was in school for four years and I had only two years, so it taught him how to speak better English. I want to talk to the people at College of DuPage, but I don't have time. My father speaks a little bit of English, but my mother doesn't speak any.

❑

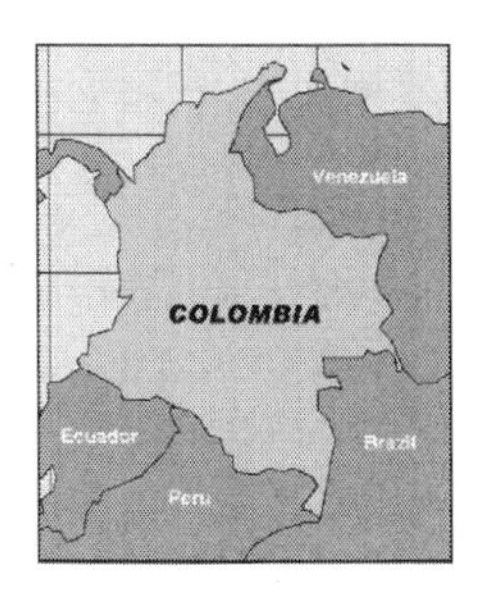

Phyllis W.

Interviewed, Spring 2014

I am a 41-year-old woman from Colombia, South America. I moved here to Illinois from Colombia eight years ago, and I currently live here with my son, husband, and most of the time, my daughter. Growing up in Colombia, I only had one sibling, a brother who is three years older, and lived almost solely with him and my mother. I also lived with my father when I was young, but when I was around the age of seven, he left to be with another woman and to start a whole new family. My father had another son, who now lives in New York City and has two children of his own. My first marriage was not much better than my mother's. Sixteen years ago, I got pregnant with my daughter and married her father. However, he was not a good husband, and we had a poor marriage. After six years of marriage, I divorced him and went back to live with my mother since my brother had moved out of the house and got married before I had married.

When I went back to live with my mother, I met my current husband within the month. He was from Colombia, but had been living in the United States for over twenty-seven years. He had only come back to Colombia for a vacation and to see the family he had left behind. We met by chance since I had just come back to live with my mother when he was visiting his sister, my mother's neighbor. After speaking with him, I learned he was a contractor, but currently he works as a truck driver for the post office. However, although it was and is wonderful that I met my current husband when living with my mother, I feel as if I met him too soon. Although I did not know it yet, our meeting, so shortly after my divorce, would have some horrible repercussions.

Although I have lived in the United States for eight years, as well as have been married to my second husband, my early years were not easy. Since being brought to the United States on a Thursday eight years ago and being married the following day, I have had some issues with my former husband. When I went to live in Illinois to be with my fiancé, who is now my husband, I left my daughter reluctantly behind with her father to finish the school year since I believed it was unfair to take her out of school during the school year. However, while I was in the United States, my ex-husband found out back home in Colombia that I had been seeing my current husband just a month after I left him, and he accused me of being unfaithful and believed that I left him to be with my current husband. Due to this belief, he thought that he had the right to keep our daughter and refused to let her come to the United States when she finished the school year. When I found out, I was furious. I hired lawyers to try to sue him for custody of my daughter and had to wait ten months for my Green Card to process so that I could go and try to retrieve my daughter since the original plan was for her to fly to the United States. Those ten months were agony since my daughter was so upset and wanted to see her mother.

When I was finally able to go back to Colombia — after I received my permanent residency card in the United States — I fought my former husband for custody, but the battle was hard and long, and I had to go back to the United States before retrieving my daughter due to the fact that I was pregnant. I left my lawyer in charge in Colombia and flew back to the United States. However, when I came back to the United States to get an ultrasound, I was given more bad news. When the doctor conducted my ultrasound, it was revealed that there was something wrong with the baby's chromosome development.

The doctor informed me that the baby would die sometime in utero or soon after birth. I was devastated, and when I was five-and-a-half months pregnant, my child died. What was worse was that I had to give birth to my dead child since I was so far along. However, there was some light in my terrible day. That same day, my lawyer called me and said that I had won the case; I was getting my daughter back after thirteen long months. Yet, I had to wait another seven months to see her since her papers to come to the United States had to be processed again because so much time had passed since they were originally filed. Eventually, after twenty months of struggle, I was able to go back to Colombia and bring my daughter to the United States. This was the last time I have been back in my home country, which was five years ago.

As for my education and work experience, in Colombia, I studied to be a secretary for two years and worked as one for nine years. As I worked, I went to a university in Colombia to study occupational health, but left after two semesters. I loved going to school and did well in my studies, but I had to drop out because I could not financially afford it anymore. When I first came to the United States, I worked in a home day care with a friend. However, I stopped working at that job and became a babysitter. When I worked as a babysitter, I became pregnant with my son. After trying to care for my son and work for the family, I decided to quit because it became too difficult to balance both. Also, my employer's attitude was poor, and the children I worked with fought a lot. After quitting that job, I began to teach Spanish classes for some time and then was hired to create examinations in Spanish for students to take. Eventually, I stopped teaching Spanish classes because I was making more money developing Spanish tests, and I could do it seasonally.

In the United States, I also obtained my phlebotomy license from a center for health education. However, I have not been able to use it because I have yet to be hired. I do, however, hope I can use it in the future and am currently studying to obtain my GED since the United States does not recognize my high school diploma. I did not realize that not having my GED in the United States would be a problem until I tried to apply for secretarial jobs. They overlooked my years of experience and only seemed to care about me having my GED from this country.

Since moving to the United States, my country, Columbia, and specifically, my home town, have changed dramatically. Although the town I grew up in is still small, it has become the second largest tourist city in Colombia. Many tourists come and take tours of the coffee plantations and beautiful parks. All my friends and family back home always say they see tourists all over the city. One of the reasons it has changed so much and has inspired tourists to visit is because of an earthquake that occurred in 1999. In the earthquake, half the city was destroyed. However, the local people were able to raise the city up from the ashes, causing many in Colombia to call it the miracle city. The city is even better than it was before the earthquake since it is full of new buildings and other structures. However, even though the earthquake was able to, in a sense, bring new life to the city, many others lost theirs. A friend of mine lost her life in the earthquake since she lived in a part of town that was not as well built as others. When the earthquake hit, the roof fell in. However, just as the roof was about to fully collapse, my friend who was holding her baby threw her child to her husband before being crushed to death. Although she died, the rest of the family survived, including her baby. On a happier note, the country itself has also changed greatly. It is no longer as dangerous as it once was and is a very popular tourist destination.

Although I moved to the United States, my brother decided to remain in Colombia. He still lives there with his wife and is doing well. He currently lives in the city next to the one that we grew up in. However, although my brother wants to remain in Colombia, my mother does not. About a month ago, she was approved by the government to come to the United States to live with my husband, children, and me. Until she moves here for good, I will continue to call her every day and Skype her when I can.

Even though my mother will be coming to the United States, I would still like to go back to Colombia to visit someday. Currently, my daughter, who is fifteen, is in Colombia. For the last four years, my daughter has not been able to go back and see her father. She was supposed to go back each summer, but for the last four years, she has had to take summer classes, causing her to not be able to go back to Colombia. However, last August, she had to go back to Colombia to have some necessary dental work done because it is cheaper there. Since being in Colombia, she has had to have surgery on her teeth, delaying her journey home. She is currently taking classes and will be back in October.

Since being in the United States, the biggest difficulty I have faced has been the language barrier. I had never had to learn English in Colombia making picking up the language a challenge. In order to learn English when I first arrived, I went to the College of DuPage to take classes for a year and a half. I am also currently taking classes online through a college in Colombia in order to better my English. As for the People's Resource Center, I came to the center not to better my English but to have help with gaining my GED. A friend of mine told me about the Center when I wanted a little help with the whole GED process, and my whole experience with the Center has been wonderful. They have been very helpful, and all the volunteers are very friendly. I am currently taking classes at the People's Resource Center in order to get my GED, and I hope to have it very soon.

❑

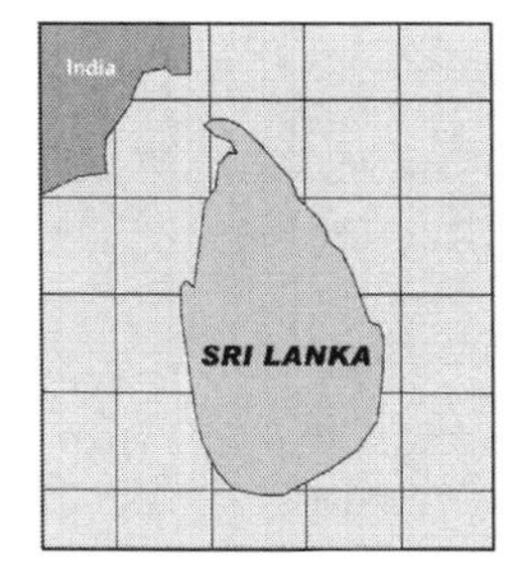

George D.

Interviewed, Spring 2014

I am fifty-four years old and was born in Sri Lanka. My mother was born in southern India, but she has no birth certificate. My father was born in a town near Kandy, Sri Lanka. I have a younger sister and an older brother; I also had a younger brother, who passed away when he was only thirty days old.

At that time, Sri Lanka was called Ceylon by the British. It has been renamed after independence. My parents were married when my mother was thirteen years old, but they have no marriage certificate. Their fathers were very religious.

I used to go to school at night. The school was called CMS for kindergarten through fourth grade and later another school; and I still have my graduation certificates.

When I was eleven, the Electric Board told us we had to move because they were going to flood the valley in order to produce more power for the area and we moved to the hills nearby.

Experiencing servitude

After we moved, when I was twelve, a friend of my father told him that I was of age and should go to work as a live-in "servant boy" to help someone else's household with cooking, cleaning, and cleaning clothes. I was paid fifteen rupees each month (U.S. fifteen cents) for my work. The boss was a madam who was not respectful of me. I was considered like the dust on the floor. For food, she pushed leftovers into my plate. She was always angry and usually forgot to give me tea at tea time. I was so poor and hungry that I would pick food from the garbage. Also, I would get my feet stepped on or my arms pinched if I did not do what the madam wanted. The scars on my arm are still visible today. To wake me in the morning, she would kick me. After a few years, when my father came to visit, I stood behind the madam when he was facing her (so she could not see me) and showed him a sign that I would kill myself if he did not take me out of there.

Getting an education and various jobs

After leaving the job as a servant boy, I joined my sister who was studying at Lakpahana Adventist Seminary in Mailapitiya (outside Kandy). It was a high school.

Right after the seminary, I lived and worked in Colombo, the capital of Sri Lanka. I worked at construction; I worked in a factory that made potato chips; and I worked in a Chinese restaurant as a cook, dishwasher, and waiter.

When thinking back to my childhood, one of my earliest memories was from my house. Once, I was a naughty boy and my uncle tied me to a post for not listening. I also remember one time my friend and I were playing at a day-care center on a mound of dirt sliding down the side; it was very dusty — I remember that. Overall, and before working at the house as a servant boy, I remember my childhood as being very happy.

As a teen at the seminary, I remember the principal was an American. He would go back to the United States and raise money for the school. He was honest and touched my heart. He was a good principal. We used to stay in contact; he lives in the Smokey Mountains now.

Before coming to the United States, I was a dog groomer in Hong Kong. I also worked in a dry cleaner and part-time cleaning houses — my ironing was the best.

I was married in July 1995. In 1998, I was working in Hong Kong at a dry cleaner and was also working for a Japanese consulate official. I sent my wife back to Sri Lanka when she was pregnant.

Journey to the United States, but without my family

I was thirty-nine years old when I came to the United States. I was sponsored by the Japanese consul in Chicago when he got posted to the United States and I went with him and his family to work in the house for his wife and two children. Soon after, he had to move back to China for a reposting, but I did not want to move back, and he asked his friend to find me a job with a doctor's family in Oak Brook. He is a surgeon and his son is an attorney. I met the doctor and his family and, since 1999, I have worked for his son, who is a quadriplegic and in a wheelchair because of a spinal injury.

Over the years, I had the ability to travel and visit my family — which had not been living with me in the United States. My oldest daughter was born in 1999, and my youngest daughter was born in

2006. It was not until August 2011 that I brought them to the United States. Today, my mother lives in Florida, but my father passed away in 1984.

I do miss Hong Kong: the food, friends, and the city itself. Also, the buses and mass transportation are first rate.

As for difficulties in the United States, I never really had any. I can speak English and I enjoy the food everywhere I go.

I became associated with the PRC through my employer, the attorney. Before my family arrived, I stayed with him. He worked in DuPage County at the court house in Wheaton along with his colleague, the daughter of one of PRC's staff members. She suggested to my employer that I could take some classes at the PRC for computers and general orientation. He had volunteered at the PRC as well.

I have personally used the computer, reading, clothing, and food pantry services. Everyone at the PRC is very nice. They are patient and helpful. My tutor at the Westmont PRC helps me to read and use the computer; she is patient with me. I have even taken a friend to study at PRC. When I called about him, right away a time to help was arranged.

I am so very proud of my family. PRC helped me to learn to read and write English; this helps me and my family every day here. PRC staff and volunteers are still helping me even now. I am in the process of applying for U.S. citizenship. PRC helped me to find the teacher for citizenship classes and also introduced me to World Relief. It takes $700 to apply for citizenship, and they helped me with qualifying for a waiver from PRC.

All I can say is that I am so appreciative of the people who started the PRC. I pray for them. They help people with food and clothing, and the people who work here make me full of joy: they are kind, lovely, patient, and respectful.

Interviewer's Note: Our interview was conducted in two parts due to his scheduling demands. He is extremely family oriented and needed to pick up his daughter from school. The first part was conducted at the Westmont PRC; the second part was conducted later in the day at a Dunkin' Donuts in Westmont. At the second session, he brought many items: maps, old pictures, an old passport, certifications, and records, which he wanted to share.

❑

Economic Considerations

This segment includes the experiences of those who have not been victims of wars, discrimination, or torture. They came to the United States to better their economic situation and provide a better education for their children. Some felt that this was not possible in their own countries because of depressed economies or lack of access to good schools and higher-paying jobs. Some were well educated in their own countries, while others had little or no education. Still others came because their parents or spouses wanted to migrate.

One person is here, not for her own sake, but because she wants to get the educational background necessary to help children in her own country.

While they have not dealt with the traumas faced by many of those who came as refugees, these immigrants do not have an automatic legal status. Some arrived undocumented and their difficulties started after they arrived. All are willing to work hard and to do anything to gain citizenship. Those who came with little education are studying to perfect their English so that they can get their GED and pass citizenship examinations.

As in all our stories, the people feel that they had to work hard for everything. They had to learn how to drive a car at an older age and navigate the new culture's daily life without much English. These obstacles made it difficult to find a job. With their parents' help and hard work, the children have been successful. This has made the parents proud, but they have come to feel that the next generation is more interested in short-term gains than long-term goals.

❑

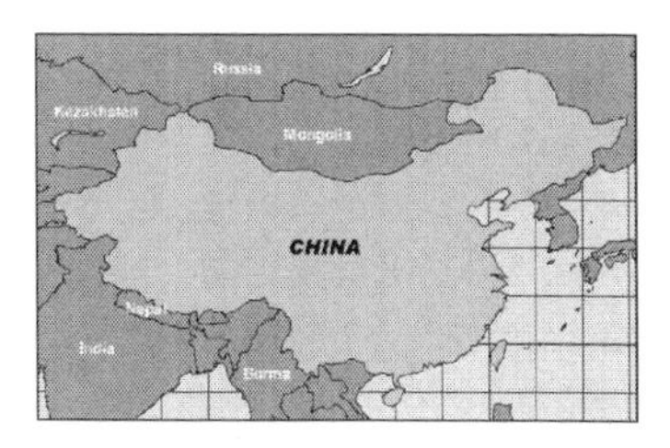

Eileen G.

Interviewed, Spring 2014

I was born in China, but have visited England, France, and Canada, before I came to the United States in 2003. I lived what I would consider a regular Chinese lifestyle. As a child of two parents who worked in good electric companies, I easily found my place in society. As I was growing up, my family moved twice. We moved into different condos; each one was through my parent's job; each condo we moved into was better than the last. My childhood was uneventful; the only memorable aspect was when my brother went to work on a farm because of the Cultural Revolution. Many young adults went to work on the farms after high school. He was gone for two years and during this time I became very spoiled, as the youngest and only girl in the family. When I was a teenager I was not as good as I should have been; often times teachers were mad at me because I was lazy. One time in gym class I did not want to follow the rules. We had to jump onto boxes and continue to jump onto the highest one. In my class I was able to jump the highest and when my teacher asked me to show the class I refused. I was shy and didn't want to show off. Then the teacher offered, if I would jump, he would let the whole class go early. So I did, and my classmates were happy, because we could all go home early. Another time in my music class, we would all just sit around and talk to each other. The teacher was upset that no one would sing to the music. My classmates asked me to conduct the class, and we all got a little out of hand. We were shouting the lyrics to the songs, giggling, and laughing. When the song ended we stopped, and when the teacher played another song we refused to sing again. Then when I began to conduct the class everyone started to sing all off tune and loud again. When class was over, a student in one of the other classes in my grade overheard the teacher talking about how he was mad, because I had conducted the class. It was not my job or place too. I eventually apologized to the teacher.

When I got my first job I was eighteen years old. I worked in a fabric company where I sat at an electric switchboard converting the energy from one section of the factory to the other. There were times when the factory could use more energy than other times, but during peak hours, we had to use less electricity. For one year I was sent to get extra electronic training at a higher education school. The school specialized in training people that did my job. The school was like a university but smaller. While I worked in the company I still lived with my parents until I got married and had my child. While I was at work there was a lot of downtime; I learned how to knit, and sometimes I would take naps. Work became very relaxing especially as opposed to being at home. When I was at home I had to do chores and run errands. At my job an average work week consisted of working four days twenty-four hours. The first day I would work for twelve hours, go home, and sleep. Then the next night I would work for twelve hours and get the next two days off. When I left my job I was thirty-nine and moving to the United States.

Before I came to the United State I had visited several times. I traveled to the United States because of my husband. My husband is a very intelligent man, he has a master's from China, a PhD from England, and has taught at the University of Ohio as a geology professor. He now owns his own environmental business. My husband came to the United States two years before me. However, I had traveled back and forth many times before settling down with him. When I left for the United States my mother was very sad. She tried to bargain with me, saying that I could live in another city in China and not have to live in a city in the United States so far away. None of my mother's begging worked; I immigrated to the United States. In America I was helped a lot by my husband, and I am still trying to learn how to do everything independently. For the first two years while living in the United States, my husband and I went everywhere together. We would go to shops together because it was easier for me. My husband was able to communicate for me because his English is better than mine.

Language has been the biggest difficulty for me. It has been one of the biggest culture shocks I faced. Hardly anyone in the United States speaks or even reads Mandarin. Learning English can really help me do everyday things. During the first months, I could not even read how much money we had in our bank account; if I wanted to open a bank account I couldn't. Everything was very hard. There are also a lot of cultural differences that I have had to overcome in the United States. One of the first times I would walk around my neighborhood, people would always say "hi" or "how's it going?" as I walked passed them. I would always look at them weird or pass them and not say anything because I didn't know how they knew me. In China if you don't know someone you don't say anything. Here it is much different. As soon as I realized that they were just being nice and nothing really more, I began to reply to them. I didn't intend to seem mean I just didn't understand. There have also been differences when being a guest at a friend's home. In China when someone first offers you something in their home you reject whatever they are trying to give you. After a while they will offer you the same thing again and that is when you accept what they are giving you. In America it is just not the same. Once I went to a friend's house, they asked me if I wanted something to drink or eat. Like in China I rejected what they offered me. However, they never offered it to me again the rest of the time I was there. I was not expecting it to be such a difference, but it was. There is also a difference in the apparel. The clothes people wear are really casual in the United States compared to China. The styles are very different too.

Since I left China there have been many changes. Once a year I go and visit my family in China. Sometimes when I go back I can't find my house. Since I left there has been a large road system built. There are huge buildings; they have destroyed the old and built everything new. The electricity also goes very fast now. It is really crazy how different everything looks.

I learned about the People's Resource Center through a friend. I use the ESL Program. Previously I had used the services at College of DuPage, but when the program ended I wanted more experience in learning English. At the People's Resource Center it has been easier for me to learn everyday conversation. In the ESL Program we talk to each other in English and work more on conversations rather than learning vocabulary words. The program has really helped me learn.

My son graduated from the University of Illinois in Champaign as an electrical engineer, and he worked in the engineering field. His boss told him that the company would pay for his master's degree if he stayed for two years. But he switched jobs and now works in the computer field. I would still like him to get his master's degree.

❑

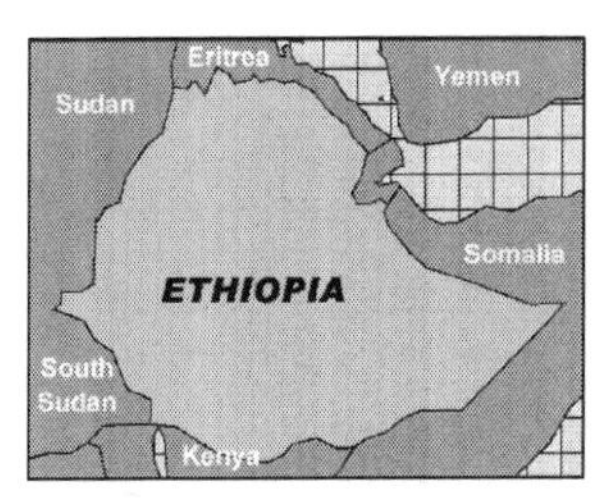

Emily P.

Interviewed, Spring 2014

I am nineteen years old. I have gone to high school in DuPage County since freshman year. I was born in Ethiopia, East Africa, and I miss it. The climate is much different; the summer there isn't as hot as here. I lived in a suburb; I went to school down there too. I have three brothers and three sisters. I am the only child from my mother's side. I'm the only child that's here in Illinois; the rest of my siblings are still in Ethiopia with the exception of one brother who is in Arizona living with my aunt. When I came, I had difficulty with the language. I came here with my mom to get a better life and education, not because of any war in Ethiopia. When we came here we had no one. Some Ethiopian and Eritrean people helped us a lot. We had an apartment ready for us. It was a very long process to come here and a lot of paper work.

I am the oldest of my siblings. I never worked outside of my home. I went to school. My favorite thing to do in Ethiopia was playing with my friends. I still keep in contact with them. I want to go back soon, but I have to go to college and finish. My mom works at a local college as a kitchen cleaner. Before coming here, my mother was in a refugee camp in Ethiopia. The language was the biggest difficulty; the school was very different. On my second day I took the wrong bus and it took me to a middle school instead of high school. I made a lot of friends here from different countries. I like my high school; my favorite subjects were math and chemistry, but now I really like English, I have a very nice teacher. I have a few friends that come to the People's Resource Center for English. I initially came with my mom in the summer and would come four to five times a week. The People's Resource Center has helped me a lot. I was shy when I first started coming here, but now I am more comfortable.

I love Ethiopia a lot, because I was born there and my entire family was there. There are more than seventy different languages and different cultures in Ethiopia, so not everyone speaks the same language. In my free time I like to go to bible study and I love to read the bible. Also, I like to go shopping with my friends on the weekend. Last summer my friend and I worked at UPS; it was a great experience. The scariest thing that has happened to me while living in the United States was when I got pulled over by an officer for the first time. I was driving and trying to learn with my mom, but she didn't have a license and I didn't either. I didn't know the rules, so the police officer gave both of us tickets, but they dismissed mine in court and I was so happy. We got to the United States by the World Relief Organization. I want to be a nurse, that's what I want to do when I graduate from high school.

❑

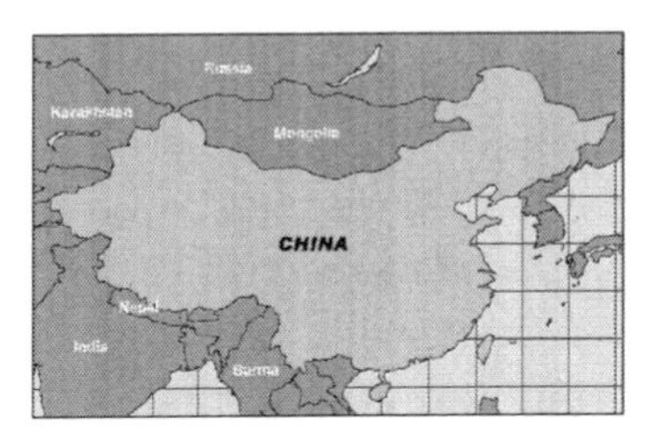

Barbara D.

Interviewed, Spring 2014

I am a 25-year-old from rural southern China where I lived with my parents and my older sister until I came to the United States with my husband at the age of twenty-one. During my time in China, I only attended school until about middle school. I never attended high school or college. I did not feel that school was for me and did not want to continue it any further. However, I was still able to obtain a job in China as a cashier; I would sell tickets to people so that they could take the ferry across a river in China. Although I did eventually come to the United States with my husband, I loved my childhood and growing up in my small rural countryside town. The area was very poor when I grew up, but each family had enough to survive. In my family, my father was a bricklayer, and my mother was a farmer. My sister and I grew up on the farm that my mother worked on, and we lived in the same town that my father had lived in all his life. My mother had grown up in another small countryside town, but had to move to live with her husband since it was customary to do so in China. Also, since my town was so small, every person in the town knew each other and it felt like living in a community. Many of the people in the town even came from the same ancestors, and although I did not grow up with a religion or with much money, I never felt as if I was missing anything as an adolescent.

As stated before, I came to the United States with my husband in 2009 at the age of twenty-one. We moved to the United States since he is an American, and we felt that the United States would be a better place to raise children. Although my husband is an American, I had met him in China since I had never left the country before coming to Illinois. He was a teacher in China who taught children English. When we came to DuPage County, we lived with my in-laws for three and half years. I loved living with my in-laws, and they were very helpful since moving away from my life in China was difficult. However, more recently, my husband, my son, and I moved out of my in-laws' house. Since moving from my in-laws' house, my husband continues to be a teacher and teaches Chinese to students in Chicago.

I also have a job working seasonally.

Although I left China almost five years ago, I have been able to go back and visit my parents and my sister. I like to go back to China to not only see my family, but to also have my son visit China and his relatives. I want my son to still have a connection to China, and my husband and I have been teaching him Chinese at home. However, although we only speak Chinese in the home, so that he will learn the language, and only have him watch Chinese programs on television, he usually speaks back to us in English even when we address him in Chinese. My husband and I also only cook Chinese food for my son and us at home since we prefer to eat it versus American food and prefer to cook it for our son. To continue his Chinese education as well as expand his knowledge of China and visit his family, my husband and I plan to continue to take him to China every year if we can afford it. We also plan to take our daughter who is on the way and due in May, the same month that our son will be turning three.

Although by American standards I married young at the age of twenty-one, in China, it is very common to be married quite young, especially in the area where I grew up. Although one has to be twenty before they can marry in China, many young adults will actually form families earlier and start having kids before they can be married. This is due mostly to the environment in which they live and Chinese traditions. Since everyone has been getting married so young in rural areas of China for so long, every generation has continued this tradition. Also, since many of the people living in the countryside of China are farmers or work strenuous jobs, many of the older generations must stop working at a younger age because of the type of hard labor they are doing. Families also need more children to help them with the labor, causing families to be started earlier and for more children to be born in many rural families.

Even though I am having a wonderful life here in the United States, I also loved living in China, and I miss my family very much. Leaving my family was the hardest part about coming to the United States. Although I was never forced to leave my home or forced to come to the United States, I still continue to miss my family. I, however, Skype my sister almost every day, which helps a little. She just had a baby even though, as the youngest, I am about to have my second child. The reason that she only recently had a child and settled down later than I did was because she went to college. She received an automotive degree, which in China authorizes her to work with machines. In the end, although I miss my family and had difficulty leaving them, as well as finding a job in the United States, which was the second hardest part of coming to the United States, I still believe that I lived a happy life and have no plans on moving back soon. However, I may move back in the distant future; it just depends on where life takes my family and me.

Since I moved to the United States in the late 2000s, China has changed greatly, especially in the area where I grew up. What I have noticed every time that I have gone back to my hometown is that the people living in the town are less poor than when I was younger. Roads have been introduced to my small town as well as cars. When I was younger, no one in my town had a car, and everything had to be carried by hand. However, now many of the families own an automobile, making life in the town a lot easier. There is also more industrial development in my hometown as well as in the major cities such as Shanghai. More buildings have sprung up, and there is more wealth. However, industrialization and the changes attributed to it have affected small rural towns in China more than the big cities since the changes are more dramatic.

My life here in the United States has been a happy one, and my involvement in the People's Resource Center has helped contribute to my prosperity. When I first arrived here from China, my mother-in-law, who I was living with, introduced me to the Center. She brought me to the PRC in order for me to take English classes. These classes have helped improve my English greatly, and I really enjoy being part of the Center, which I have been coming to for almost five years. At the PRC, I have also taken some education classes in the fields of history and science as well as other subjects. The PRC greatly helped me while I prepared to take my GED, which I passed. Because of the PRC, I am now able to get better jobs here in the United States, and in a few years after my children are a little older, I plan on attending college at College of DuPage. I want to go into the medical field and hopefully take classes and train to be a physical therapist or something similar.

During my time in China, there were few big events that truly affected my family and me due to where we lived. Our rural community did not change much or was affected by many of the changes that occurred in other areas of China until after I had already left. I did notice, however, that over the last few years or so women have begun to gain more rights in China. Yet, many families still prefer to have male children, and I believe that even though females are starting to gain more rights and beginning to be looked at in a more positive manner, male babies will remain more desirable due to tradition. During my years in China, I also saw the "one child policy" change. (This policy was introduced in 1979 to control the immense population explosion in China, the world's most populous country.) When I was younger, if a family wanted or had more than one child, they were required to pay the government to keep the child. This caused many families to abort or abandon various "undesirable" children all over China. Being the younger of two, my parents had to pay to keep me, and my sister in the future will inherit the land my parents own while I will get nothing. In my small town, however, there were a lot of families who had multiple children, and I never observed any of them abandoning any of their children. They just paid lots of money to keep their children. When my parents were younger, each one of them also had four siblings, but during that time their parents did not have to pay. It was not until my sister and I were born that the policy affected my family. Yet, the policy has been changing. Now a couple can have two children without paying the government for the second one if both the parents did not have siblings. However, although the policy has changed, many families in China still get rid of their second child or a child they do not want.

One problem that causes so many couples to have more than one child as well as have the children younger than they may desire is the fact that sexual education is not taught in many schools. When I was younger, my teachers skipped over the sexual education lesson since the government did not encourage us to learn about our bodies. In order for me to learn about my body, I had to ask my classmates who did not know much more than I did. Living at school, which most students had to do in China from middle school on, allowed me to converse with my classmates more about the problems or questions that I had although I did not have much time to speak with them. At school each day, we had to wake up at 6:30 A.M., brush our teeth, exercise for an hour, read for a while, then go to breakfast, have class, eat lunch, have afternoon class until six, eat dinner, and then finally go to night class until around 9:00 at night. This schedule would continue on each day for ten days, which also included homework, and then finally we would have around three and a half days off in which we would go home. However, we would have winter and summer breaks in which we did not have to be at school. This type of schooling is still occurring in my home city, and although many students are learning a lot from this approach, some students are discouraged from continuing on with school. They feel as if they do not have a life, and many girls feel as if they do not have enough time to get ready for higher education. I am glad my son and later my daughter will be able to be to go to school here in the United States rather than in China.

❑

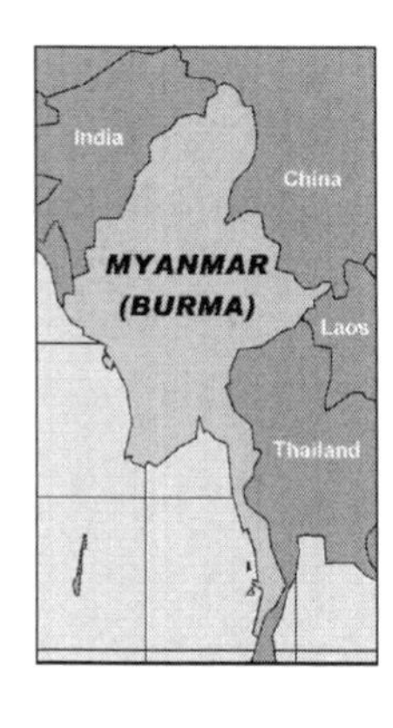

Donald L.

Interviewed, Spring 2014

I was born in Burma (Myanmar), Southeast Asia, and I am fifty-eight years old. I came to the United States fifteen years ago with my wife and children. I have been married for more than thirty years. My son is studying at a local college and intends to be a dentist. My daughter has finished school and does not live with us anymore. My family now lives in DuPage County.

In Burma, I had my own business, a grocery store. It was taken over by another person. If you didn't have a job there it was difficult to live; the rich get richer and the poor get poorer. I moved to America to further my family's education because there is equal opportunity here and also because the laws in Burma were getting really bad. I have not been back to Burma

I have three brothers and three sisters. They live in Pakistan and Germany. I made the Hajj [a pilgrimage to Mecca, Saudi Arabia, the birthplace of Mohammed and the holiest city in the Muslim world, for prayers at the holy shrine, the Kaaba] in 1984, the same year my daughter was born. I went to Pakistan in 1992 because my mother was sick. My wife has seven sisters and three brothers. My wife and I got married in 1980.

My wife's sister was in the United States so we knew someone when we got here. She helped us out a lot. My wife works at a local company and I collect Social Security because my doctors aren't letting me work. It is very hard to live off the government. We're much better off now, but still not great. My kids are mostly finished with school. I go to the mosque in DuPage County and my wife usually reads the Quran when she is at home. We take our religion to heart.

There was no need to learn English while I was in Burma, but right now I am in an English class at the College of DuPage and PRC because I need help with writing and speaking English as well as reading.

My most memorable moment when I came to the United States was when my wife and children and I flew to Thailand, then to Los Angeles, and then to Chicago. It took twenty-five hours. My son told me about the People's Resource Center and got me into English courses three years ago. The one thing I loved when I came here were the rules which say that nobody gets special treatment. I was very surprised by the weather in Chicago because of the snow and the four seasons. My biggest obstacles when I first arrived were that I had no money, no food, no house, and no medical insurance. I want to open a grocery store and have customers understand me and I understand them.

> *Editors' note:* When Sadia met the interviewee, he asked her where she was from. She told him that her parents were from Saudi Arabia and Pakistan, and he asked immediately, "Do you speak Urdu?" After she answered, "Yes," most of the interview was then conducted in Urdu.

❑

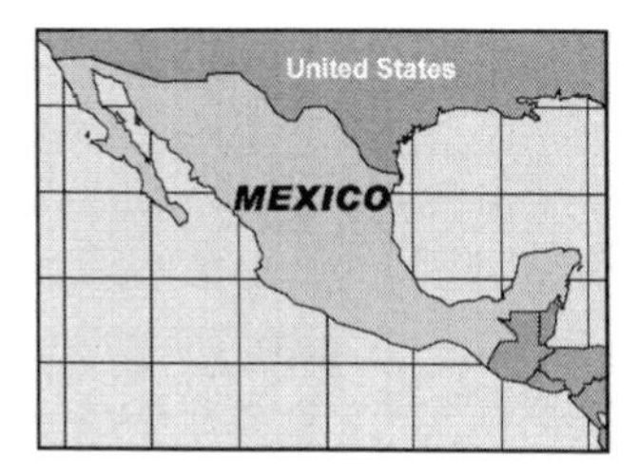

Dwayne A.

Interviewed, Spring 2014

I am a 77-year-old man from Mexico. After living in various places in Mexico, I moved to Chicago and later the Chicago metro area, where I currently live. When I was very young, my mother divorced my father. When I was about four or five, my younger brother and I moved in with my grandmother and grandfather, where I stayed until I finished primary school. My grandparents lived on a farm, and it was there that I started working for the first time. In the mornings before school, I would get up and sow corn in the fields. However, when I was around twelve, my mother married again, a man who would become my stepfather, causing us to move. My mother, stepfather, younger brother, grandparents, and I then moved to a different town in Mexico. Due to our move, we had to sell the farm.

After primary school, I went on to secondary school in this new town and then acquired a vocational degree in accounting. I was only one of a few students in my class that went on to achieve a signed vocational degree and certificate from the state. This degree certified me as a junior accountant in Mexico. One of my first jobs as an accountant had me working in a municipal building in Mexico. Later, I went on to work as an accountant in a fairly large corporation. I also worked for a bank in Mexico and a telephone company. One of my tasks in one of the many jobs that I held during my time in Mexico was to check the time cards of all the employees who would check into work every day. This was a very important task since many employees worked for this conglomerate. I was also part of a union in Mexico that secured my working rights. During this time, I also married very young, and we had two sons. However, since we had married so young, the marriage did not work out, and we divorced.

In 1959, I made my way to the United States with some friends to enter the country and to find work. Some really hard times were ahead for me. I settled in downtown Chicago where I found a job at a plant and tree nursery. However, since I was unfamiliar with the transportation system, I would walk dozens of blocks each day to work. Since I had to start work at 7:00 A.M., I would have to leave my house at 3:30 A.M. in the morning in order to make it to work in a timely fashion. After arriving at work, I would work an eight-hour shift and then walk all the way home. While working at the nursery, a friend of mine told me of a better job opening. The job was more desirable, and I would be working for an ice cream company. Sadly, the ice cream company is no longer in business today. While working in the United States, I also took welding classes in order to become a welder. Eventually, I graduated and was able to use my degree.

During the first years of my life in the United States, I met my present wife at one of the many dances that I would attend on weekends. My wife was born in Indiana to immigrants from Mexico. She is bilingual, which helped me in the United States since I did not know much English. We have been married for fifty-two years now, and we have four girls. Three live in Illinois and one in Pennsylvania. I also have more than twenty grandchildren and great grandchildren. As for my two sons from my first marriage, after I left Mexico, my mother adopted them, and they remained in Mexico for a while. However, with my help, they are now both in the United States along with my mother, who arrived with my stepfather before he died. My mother lives in Texas with one of my sons, and the other son lives in Illinois.

Even though my mother and all my children live in the United States now, and I have been a naturalized citizen since 1976, I still encountered some tough times here in the United States. When I first came to Chicago, my uncle had already been living in the area working as a meat inspector. When I came to him asking him to sponsor me, he denied me and provided me little help in the United States. Although this was a difficult experience, I learned that sometimes friends can help more than family. My friends were the ones that helped in my first years in the United States and even helped me obtain a job at a steel company. It was the boss of this company, who was from Germany, who eventually gave me a letter that allowed me to continue to work and stay in the United States and after seventeen years to become a citizen. When he interviewed me and I told him that I had no specific skills, but I wanted to work hard, he told me that this was the kind of person he was looking for. After gaining my degree in welding as well as working at this job full-time — and many others that I had in the United States — I eventually was able to gain a position in the Electric Motor Division, a part of General Motors, where I worked for thirty years before retiring.

During my time at the Electric Motor Division, I was able in 1975 to buy a house with my wife, which is the same house that we still reside in today. After taking a sixth-month construction course at the College of DuPage, I knocked down the original house that stood on my property and built a better one. Eventually, when a complex was built near my house, the inspector of the complex admired how well built my house was and that it was built even better than the new complex. I did all the work alone with help from my friends, besides the electricity and the plumbing. In 1978 at the Electric Motor Division, someone came in and taught me how to use computers for the first time. Eventually, I was able to move up in the company. I began as welder and then moved to a lineman. From there, I worked in shipping and receiving. Even after retiring in 1993, however, I still worked part-time at School District 66.

It was not until many years after being in the United States that I came to the People's Resource Center. For years, my wife helped me along with English. We spoke to each other in Spanish, and although I knew a few words and phrases in English, I would still need my wife's help on some occasions. Many times she would translate things for me, causing me to never fully learn English. Eventually, I came to the People's Resource Center to learn English. The classes really helped improve my English. At the PRC, I am also now taking computer classes in order to improve my computer skills further. Since the People's Resource Center has been so helpful, I am now also volunteering at the PRC.

> *Editors' Note:* The interviewer met with Dwayne a second time and he brought with him documentation about his many career changes. Like so many of the other interviewees, Dwayne represents the immigrants who overcame many obstacles to become very successful: he entered as an undocumented person and became a citizen because he convinced people that he wanted to work and they sponsored him. He retrained, and retrained himself many times and received certificates, among them: UAW Leadership Training Institute; different levels of welding skills; auto mechanic; automotive engine testing; and small engine service and repair. He became active in the union movement and was the director of a credit union for eight years. He took classes at the Education Center to teach people about unions (and to

dispel stereotypes) and then became active in politics as a precinct registrar for signing up voters. He also went back to his training as an accountant in Mexico: he became a public notary and certified tax accountant.

❑

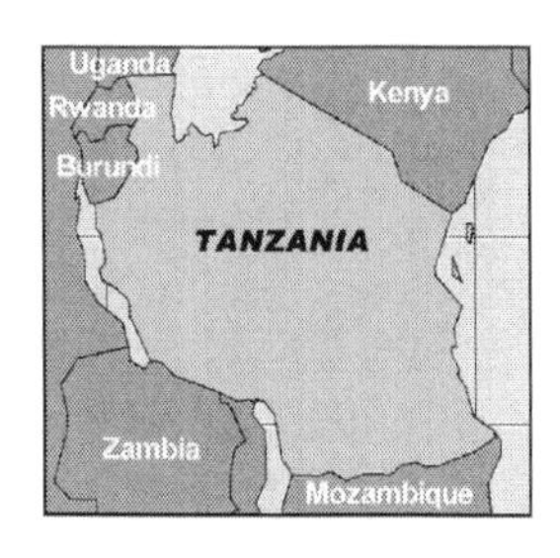

Sr. Teresa J.

Interviewed, Spring 2014

I was born and raised in Tanzania, East Africa. I am from a small family: my mother, father, sister, and myself. My sister has three children, one daughter and two boys, one of them who can't walk because he had polio. My sister has a hard time to take care for her son. My sister is a nurse in a small village. She works in the government dispensary. She works very far from our parents. If our parents become sick, our relatives take care of them.

As I grew up I lived in a small village of about 300 people; my childhood was a mixture of happiness and sadness. In my life I experienced poverty. In Tanzania, while some people are rich, many people have nothing and they come from nothing. My parents are small farmers. They grow maize, beans, sunflowers, cassava, and sweet potatoes. They grow the crops for their food and they sell some of the maize and beans. When I was at home I helped my mother to fetch some water and to cook. We had a small kitchen, and we used firewood to cook. I had to collect firewood from the forest and carry it on my head. We got some water from the river so I had to take a bucket down to the river and fetch the water and carry twenty liters (5.3 gallons) on my head. That is the life for all people in my village. The people in my village speak Pangwa, our local language.

My childhood was mainly happy, but due to the custom that men could have more than one wife, my mother became the second wife of my father. He already had a wife with many children. This meant that whatever he earned, he shared with the two families, and he wasn't at home many nights when he visited the other family. My mother basically had to earn her own upkeep and provide for us. Because my mother could not provide for both of us, my sister moved away and stayed with relatives who paid for her education. In a way, I was lucky, because we were just a small family. I felt that my father cared more for his other family, especially since he had to spend more money on them because there were more of them. I am sure they felt the same. This is one aspect that is not often talked about when polygamy is allowed and practiced. It made it also difficult for me to understand, since both my parents were Catholic and my mother suffered greatly from it.

My mother worked so hard for me to go to school; she was always working to get money and food for us to eat. I started primary school when I was nine years old because the school was very far from home. When I studied in primary school I had to walk about three kilometers [two miles] to school. I had to wake up early in the morning in order to get to school early, because if I was late the teachers beat me. I didn't like school because of the punishment from the teachers. But my mother encouraged me. When I returned from school I found her home and she had already food for me. In school we studied the Swahili language. When students study English it is very difficult because when they go home they speak the local language or some of them speak Swahili. Sometimes even teachers don't know English and they have to teach English. That is the big problem of English in my country.

We had a small school dispensary with one or two nurses and they didn't have medicine. If we went to that dispensary we would just get an aspirin to reduce a fever. While in primary school we had to work on the farm. We had a big school farm of maize. We had grown some maize for our lunch and some was sold to pay our school fees. I remember when I studied in the primary school the school fee was twenty shillings, but most of the parents didn't have the money to pay it. That's why we had to grow maize. During the farm work, if we were not working hard we got punished. I liked to study mathematics but our math teacher was very crazy. He was a drunk. Sometimes he just beat students as if they were cows. I did not like him so I didn't understand his lesson. I liked playing with my classmates. Sometimes we went to swim in the river. That river was very big and dangerous. Some people had died in that river, but we were not afraid.

After seven years of primary school, I took the national examination and I passed. I went to secondary school when I was fifteen years old, in a government school. The life in that school was very difficult because it was a day school and some of my classmates and I had to rent a house. The house was not good because the roof was made of grass. When it rained water got inside the room. We constantly moved beds to find a dry place. We were four students in this small house. The house had two bedrooms and a living room. My parents had little money to pay for tuition and rent. Sometimes I missed classes while helping my parents get money for my school. Every weekend I had to walk about five kilometers [three miles] to my parents to get food, because in that school every student had to cook her own food. It was very difficult to study and at the same time to prepare the food. I used to eat ugali [corn meal] and beans every day. Sometimes when my mother had some money she bought some fish for me. I used to eat some rice and chicken, but only at Christmas and Easter time because it was very expensive. In our school we had no books, only the teacher had a book; the students had to listen and write notes. At the end of four years we had the national examination, but I didn't do well because of my hard life in that school. I finished secondary school when I was nineteen years old.

When I was in senior year, I wrote a letter to join a convent. I used to know the Sisters because they came to my parish to preach and teach catechism to the kids. And I saw some Sisters from my village when they came to visit their parents. I went to visit their convent and wanted to join them. I asked my parish priest to help me to write the letter to the convent. After one month I got the letter from the vocational director to inform me that they were happy to have received my letter so they wanted me to join them as soon as I finished my classes. My mother was very happy. After I finished my classes and had passed my national examination I went to join the community as a candidate. I was very happy to join the new group of girls. They were very kind and joyful. They always made me happy; however, I missed my parents and my friends. Everything in the convent was different from my home, so I had to learn a new life and make new friends. After two years I became a postulant. During that time I learned to sew the nun's clothes. Also I was ringing the bell to remind the sisters of the time of prayers. At that time we had to study the bible and church history. After two years as a postulant, I became a novice in 1999, with a veil and a new name. At that time we had to pray and study the Rule. During the novice time we had to decide if we wanted to make vows or not. When I was a novice I worked in the chapel, decorating, cleaning, and preparing for mass. After one year as a novice I went to live in a parish for six months as a time of practicing work and prayer. During that time I worked in the chapel and visited the sick and elderly people. I was taking food and clothes to the people who didn't have food and clothes. We prayed together in their homes.

After my return to the convent, I took my first vows, which was an important event in my life. Both my parents came, but because my father had two wives, he couldn't receive communion, which made me ashamed. It was the first time that I had seen them in six years. After one year in the convent to learn the life of a religious Sister, I joined a teacher's college. Right after I finished college I went to live in a parish with a group of five Sisters and two priests. I was a teacher in a government primary school. The parish, which is a mission station of the convent, was about one hundred kilometers [sixty-six miles] from the convent. The parish served thirty-two small churches, about fifty miles from the main church. During the week, the Sisters worked in the dispensary, in the sacristy, or were teaching. On Sundays, we accompanied the priests to the outlying churches. The teachers received a small stipend from the government, and we had four cows, a bull, and two calves, and raised chickens, rabbits, and pigs for our own use, and we sold eggs and milk. We also grew maize, beans, peas, and tea plants. We had a communal TV, but often no electricity.

I taught from 2004 till 2007 when I made final vows. It was very difficult for me to teach because of many students in that school. We had about 600 students for nine teachers. The students were from around the village. The students' parents were involved in planting trees for timber and tea plants. Many of the parents spent their money on alcohol and didn't care about their children's education. We had to teach in crowded classes. When I went in one class I found about ninety-five students. I didn't believe that I could teach in that crowded class and make sure they understood the lesson. The students didn't have books; only the teacher had a book, so I had to read and explain what the lesson was about. At the end of the period I had to write notes, the students copied them, and I marked their papers. I had to teach from the third to the seventh grade. I was teaching science, social science, civics, Kiswahili, and math. The big problem was who could teach English? English is a difficult language, even to the teachers. While teaching I also had to take care of our cows and pigs at the convent. We had one worker for cows and goats and one worker for pigs and a small garden, where we got vegetables for our livestock. Every day after classes I had to ensure that all animals were safely locked in the barn and had eaten. During the weekend I was helping the workers to feed the animals, clean the barn, and plant the vegetables in our garden.

In January 2012, my superior called me and said I had a scholarship in America. It was like I had dreamed a dream. I wasn't sure if it was true. After four months I got a passport, and in August 2012, I was accepted by a local university in Illinois. So I had to get prepared for an interview. Always I was thinking about an interview because I knew that my English was poor, but I asked God to help me. I had an appointment to be interviewed at the U.S. Embassy in August. I was the first person to be interviewed that day and I was interviewed by a woman. I asked her if I could speak in Swahili, but she said, "No, you have to speak English." I said, "I am not good in English so it will be difficult to understand you." She said, "I will speak slowly so you will understand me." So she started to ask questions. I remember two questions she asked: "How did you know about that school?" and "Why do you want to study in America?" It was very difficult for me to answer in English, but God helped me and I passed the interview and got a visa.

I left Tanzania in September 2012 by Swissair from Dar es Salaam to Nairobi and Zurich and got to Chicago the next day. I was very afraid when the plane was taxiing down the runway and at the time when the plane took off, since this was my first flight. On the way I had trouble with food. I didn't know what kind of food it was that I got on the airplane. When the flight attendant asked me what kind of food I wanted to eat, I asked for chicken and what they gave me was a different kind from the kind which I had known. I stayed two hours in Zurich waiting for another plane. I didn't know even my gate number and because I was poor in English I felt embarrassed to ask. I thought they will be laughing at me. I just smiled and if someone smiled at me I asked the question. That's how I found one girl and asked her if she knew the gate which I was supposed to go to and she said, "I am looking for the same gate too." I asked her, "Where are you going?" She said, "I'm going to Chicago." She said, "Just follow me and I will help you." So I got a good friend. Two of the Sisters, one also from Africa, came to O'Hare to pick me up. When I found them I was very happy. When we got to the convent, the Sisters were in the dining room for lunch. They received me with great joy and the prioress introduced me to the Sisters. When she introduced me she said, "We have been waiting for Sr. Teresa for a long time." I was very thrilled and I felt at home.

The next day, I went to Springfield to live with another order of Sisters for three months, to learn English. I had little English vocabulary so I didn't talk much. The Sisters helped me to learn English because everyone wanted to help me. One day when I was in Springfield my classmates and I went to the Abraham Lincoln museum. After I finished my tour, I started to walk home. I walked about two hours, and I realized that I was lost. I stopped and asked one woman to show me the way to the convent. She said it is very far from here so you can't walk. She asked if I have some money, I said no. She gave me some money and said you have to stay here and wait for a bus. I stayed about ten minutes, but I thought I might take a wrong bus. So I decided to walk again back to downtown and take the bus home. I walked again about two hours to downtown, and I asked another woman if she knew the bus to the convent. She was not sure which bus could I should take so she decided to take me to a bus driver and asked for help, and he took me to the bus number seven, which passed by the convent, and they dropped me off. I was very exhausted and hungry.

I started my classes in September 2012, two days after I arrived from Tanzania. At the beginning, it was very hard because of the long flight and the time change. The first day I went to my class, I found only Chinese students. I felt lonely and uncomfortable because I thought they will not be nice to me because of my color, however, they were good people, especially one girl. I will never forget her smile when she saw me for the first time. She became my best friend in the class. They loved me and I loved them. I passed the TOEFL test [a test for foreign students that allows them to take college courses for credit] on the second try in December 2012. The test was very difficult and I didn't expect to succeed. When we got our results I passed. I didn't believe my eyes that I passed. Only four students of the fourteen students passed. I left Springfield in December 2012. At the evening meal before I left the Sisters sang songs for me to wish me a Merry Christmas and Happy New Year. Also they gave me gifts and good wishes for a safe journey. Next day, early in the morning I went to the train station with my sister friends — ready for my trip to DuPage County. It was very difficult to leave them because I loved them so much.

Sister Helen came to pick me up at the Joliet train station to drive me to the convent. I enjoyed time here during my vacation before Christmas with decorating Christmas trees and arranging the flowers in the chapel. It was a new experience for me because it was a first Christmas in America. I loved the way they arrange trees and flowers because in my country we don't have flowers for Christmas we have only Christmas trees.

I like to study English because I know when I have finished my classes I will be able to teach English in my country especially to kids. I am lucky because many people would like to study English, but they don't have the chance. English is very difficult. I could not learn English without help. I would like to thank all those who helped me in Springfield and my friends who continue to help me to learn English, under the auspices of the PRC. I especially thank the Sisters here who gave and give me my daily needs. In a particular way I would like to thank Sister Helen. She is more than a mother because I remember from the first day I arrived in America she was the one I knew the first because she came to pick me up at Chicago International Airport. When I got to the convent she had given me everything I needed. Since I came here she is always ready to help .She always asks if I need something.

I know the Sisters and my other friends spend their time to help me because of their love.

I feel at home because I miss nothing here. It feels like my community in Tanzania.

Editors' note: Sr. Teresa finished her first year at the university successfully. Tutoring her made both of us (the editors) aware that people from overseas not only struggle with the language, but with cultural concepts in the political, economic, and social life that are different or nonexistent in their home country. Being surrounded by so much "newness" also leads to homesickness and a desire to be in familiar surroundings.

In our conversation with her, Sr. Teresa expressed her deep desire to help educate children who are struggling in her country. She has experienced children who go to school, walking for miles and not having eaten for perhaps a day or two. But her special interest lies in securing equal opportunities for women in education, in the job market, and in their general standing in society.

❑

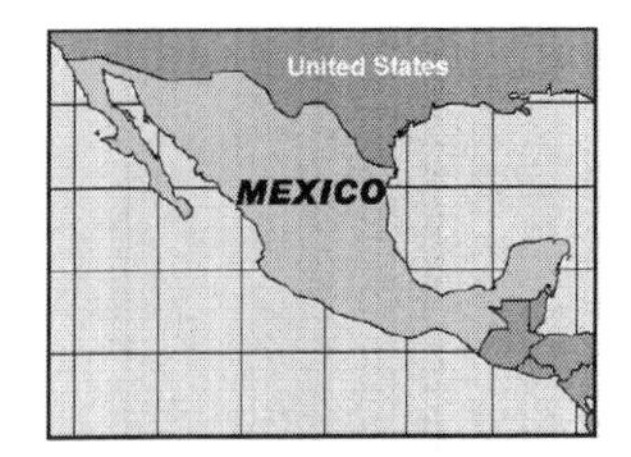

Alicia H.

Interviewed, Spring 2014

Editors' note: Alicia came to the PRC as a client and went on to become a volunteer and then a staff member.

I am in my fifties. I was born in Mexico as the oldest of ten children: two sisters and seven brothers. I grew up on a farm in a rural farming village where we raised cows, horses, chickens, sheep, and rabbits. My family was able to obtain this variety of livestock, because my father would work in different places, and as compensation he would often get animals. He was always willing to share with our neighbors; he would let them come to get milk from the cows and other things. Sometimes, my parents would sell the animals for money to pay expenses, but this was not often. Whatever we grew on our farm we would eat. Most of our meals consisted of eggs, chicken breast, cheese, and milk. My father was a very hard worker and we were better off than many in our village. When we were little we never knew if anything bad was going on; we never knew our parents' problems or what they went through. It was not the children's business to ask and it was not my parents' business to tell their children.There was also no way to know what was going on in the country. There were no newspapers, television, or radio. We only knew what was around us.

Growing up in Mexico, I lived in an adobe house which was not equipped with running water or electricity. However, these living conditions were not difficult for me because I did not know anything else. My father was able to get every child a bed to sleep in. In order to imagine the house, picture a big bedroom with five or six beds in a row for children, dirt floors, with a fireplace inside. We used our sheep's wool to make blankets to keep us warm. When we cleaned the house we would use bushes to sweep the floors.

My childhood was sometimes sad, because I wanted so badly to go to school, but it was two hours away and the trip was also too dangerous for a girl. My brothers were able to walk the distance to school, and even though I wanted to be educated, I was a girl; my job was to raise the family and get married so I could raise my own family. In our society there was no need to educate the woman. I was the one that raised my brothers; I am like a mother to them. I was never jealous of their education, however, I believed it was unfair. My parents often made me upset when I was told that I had to get married because I knew that meant I would have children. I had already raised my brothers and sisters, getting married and having my own children was not something that was attractive to me at that time. My parents never knew about this; it was how I personally felt about getting married and raising a family. I had a feeling always how my life would be different had I gone to school and not needed a man to support me. However, I was always happy to help raise my brothers so my mother could go and work in the fields. My brothers and sisters have always loved me like a mother.

I remember happy times as well. Every Sunday my parents would go into town for a Catholic mass, and they would bring home fruit and sweet rolls. We would always watch for my parents to come home and we were just so happy when they would arrive and give us some of the food from town. Those were happy times. When I met my husband I was thirteen and he was fourteen; we started dating and married at fifteen and sixteen. We always knew we wanted to leave; we didn't know that it was going to be to the United States, but we knew we would go somewhere. We chose the United States because we heard stories. We heard that when you go to the United States you can work and get paid in *dollars*, we thought, "Oh, this would be so good to get dollars." At this time one dollar was twelve pesos. We thought that it would be so easy to work and earn a living in the United States. If you work a whole day in Mexico maybe you can make twelve pesos, so it sounded really good to go to the United States and earn more. I left Mexico when I was sixteen years old.

I left in part because I got married. My husband and I lived in the same town in Mexico and when we got married we had nowhere to live. There were no jobs for us either, so we decided that we would work to get a better job. We wanted a better life than our parents so we went to America. We also wanted a better life for our children. My husband left for the United States two years before I could make the trip. In the United States he spent two years to raise enough money to bring me to America. My family didn't know that I was going to the United States; they never thought I would be brave enough to leave for America on my own. They didn't know I was going to leave Mexico until I was ready to go. My parents were very happy that I got married to a man that had such initiative and work effort, but they were sad I was leaving them. The only thing is they knew my life would be better; I would get an opportunity that I would not have had if I stayed in Mexico. I didn't want my parents to convince me to stay, even when I told them they were not upset that I was leaving. They knew I wanted a better life, and they could not deny a move to the United States because I had a husband. It was sad to leave my family. I had been so happy to leave Mexico mainly because I was finally going to be able to see my husband, who I hadn't seen in two years. There was such excitement not only to see him, but to see a different country and see different people. There was also a hope that I would make a lot of money!!

I did immigrate to America; I crossed the border illegally. It was very hard and sad journey. I traveled by bus for three days, for seventy-two hours. Then when we got to the border I stayed in a little motel where there was no water, no beds, just a little room where I stayed for two days. Then at night we crossed with another group of people. We walked for a whole night. Then we stayed in a dumpster for a while until it was time to walk again. To avoid the border guards, we walked at night to San Diego, California. I spent a week in San Diego; we then fit eleven people in a car trunk one on top of the others, and they took us to Los Angeles. In one room there were like fifty people with one bathroom. After a week or two my journey continued; somebody brought twenty-six of us in a pickup truck and gave us one bucket to do our business. It took us a very long time to get to Chicago. The travel was difficult, but when we were all traveling we were like family; we all came from the same types of places, and we all looked out for each other. When we all arrived at our destination we went our separate ways. When I got to Chicago my husband came to pick me up. My husband had arrived to the United States the same way. I would never advise someone to come to America the way I did, it just isn't safe. It can be horrific if someone loses their life and their family will never know what happened to them.

When I came to America my husband and I lived with my husband's uncle. We stayed in his basement for three years. The basement was furnished and we lived among his possessions, because it was his storage area. Living there didn't really help us financially; we still paid rent but it was all we could afford. It took me and my husband fifteen years to raise enough money to have a down payment for a house, where we have lived for twenty-five years.

Coming to the United States I was a little shocked. I thought that it would be very hard for me to communicate with the people. I thought all I would see is white people with blond hair and blue eyes, but I was mistaken. Everyone I saw for a really long time was Mexican, because those were the ones I was traveling with. And then in Chicago all the people I was dealing with were Hispanic too. It was very surreal; my husband and I stayed in West Chicago for three years and everything was Hispanic. The grocery store, the post office, everywhere I could communicate in my native language.

I found my first job in America by asking my husband to take me everywhere that was hiring, and I applied everywhere. He helped me with the little English he knew to fill out applications. My first job was in a factory for a few months. I held several factory jobs; some of the factories paid better than others. Eventually I worked for UPS, loading and unloading packages at night; during the day I would work in an office as a bilingual translator. I worked there for eight years. After that I volunteered at PRC for a couple of years and then they offered me a job where I have now been working for about sixteen years.

Nonetheless, language was a huge barrier for me when I came to America. A lot of times when I talk, even today, people tell me that they do not understand me because of my accent. I think they say they do not understand me because they do not want to deal with the language barrier. When most people understand me, then someone else says they don't understand me, I don't know why. How can some people understand me and others can't? There are times when I talk on the phone at my job and people say, "I need to speak to an American, and I say, 'I'm sorry but I am American, how can I help you?'" It is nice when people try to make an effort to communicate with me, like if they say "Hola" it is nice to see that they are at least trying to be friendly and understanding that English is a second language. There was nothing else much of a shock when coming to the United States, because my husband had been here and he had everything set up for me to live.

I was able to learn to speak English mostly through my four children. Being that I was always working they learned how to talk from the people at their day care. They didn't know Spanish; I used to ask them things in Spanish, and they would ask me to say it to them in English and that is how I learned. I was also able to learn from "Sesame Street" and "Mr. Rogers." I was sad that I was never able to read Spanish; I can read some Spanish, however I cannot understand always what it is saying. I can read better in English now.

There is one time I remember, when I lost my job, my neighbors knew I was in need. My neighbors saw that I was struggling to pay my rent, with four children, they informed me to go to the People's Resource Center to try and get help and that the People's Resource Center had a food pantry. When I went there they asked me questions: address, where do I live. And when I told them my address they asked me for my apartment number. When I told them I lived in a house they denied me access to the food, because they said that if I could afford a house then I didn't need to use the food pantry [see editors' note below]. That was the worst experience that I had because I genuinely needed the food. It was not easy to ask for help, but when you need to do it, you have to do it, so when I see people asking for help I know that it is because they really need it. I didn't want people to think that I was lazy and that is why I needed help, because I was very young and able to work. The next week I came back and asked if I could help and I started volunteering, for my compensation once a month I would get a week's worth of food. I never felt that I was getting free food. I felt good about myself because I was working for the food. I then found another job but continued to volunteer every week, because it made me feel good. I also learned a lot of English from helping. Eventually they hired me.

I always put a special emphasis for our children to get an education. Most importantly for me was that my daughters got educated. The boys if they are not smart it doesn't matter, because they are men, they are strong, and they can work to support themselves. But for my daughters, I taught them that they don't need a man to survive, that they do not have to grow up and just be a wife. You can go to school and take care of yourself; you do not need a man. If you want to get married that is ok, but you do not need to! My oldest daughter is a social worker; the other is a medical assistant. One of my sons was able to go to college, but he did not finish; the other just finished high school. They both work very hard. All of them are doing better than they would if they were in Mexico. If I had stayed in Mexico I would have probably had more than four children, but life would have been so much harder. I didn't want to live my parent's life with ten children and no schooling.

For about thirty years about once a year we usually visit my family. However, conditions are very different. It is amazing that they have now running water, electricity, and all the services that we have here. I have never regretted leaving, no matter how hard it can be to earn a living in the United States. It can be hard though not having family so close, especially on holidays and other special occasions. I do not know how someone could regret leaving because my children are most important to me, especially for them to get an education and the opportunity for a good life. When I go and visit my family in Mexico, we have huge feasts together; we eat every meal together. We all get together in my parents' house and have such a good time. I'm not sure if they always get along when I'm gone, but when I am there we all just love each other. My one niece told me that I am like magic: whenever I come to visit everyone is together. When my children used to go to Mexico with my husband they loved it; they were able to be so free. There was no type of ill feeling because of the conditions or anything. They were able to ride the horse on the farm and spend time with their cousins.

I do not consider myself an immigrant; I am a U.S. citizen, and this is my country where I have spent most of my life. I have my house here and I raised my children here, and now I am helping to raise my grandchildren here, this is my home. At the People's Resource Center I have used the food pantry, clothes closet, and ESL Program. I am now working on my GED. It took me many years to apply for a GED because I wanted to raise my family and make sure that they were well educated. Now I have free time, and once a week I see the teachers at the PRC and they have been helping me study. Biggest impact on me is the job I have with no schooling. I love America and the opportunities that I have been able to get for not only me but my children. I would not change it for anything in the world.

Editors' note: This was an unauthorized decision by an individual volunteer, contrary to the policy of the PRC. The only requirement to receive help at the PRC is proof of residency in DuPage County, according to the articles of its charter.

❑

Volunteers

We have included volunteers in our interviews because PRC is not just a service agency, but a community of clients, volunteers, and staff. Everybody is giving, but everybody is also receiving.

Nobody would volunteer for years, if they did not feel a personal connection with the clients. They feel that the clients teach them so much about perseverance, patience, and an understanding of the survival of poverty, hardships of war, and disruption of families. The volunteers feel that they are helping — even just a bit — to integrate immigrants and refugees into American society.

❑

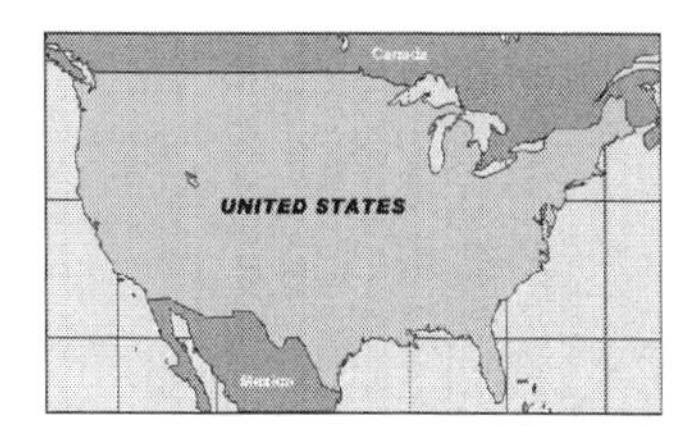

Vince Fagin

Interviewed, Spring 2014

Editors' note: Vince is retired. He is an ESL instructor at the Westmont PRC and volunteers with other organizations, such as World Relief.

I am seventy-four years old, retired, and a volunteer with many organizations. I was born in Missouri, but I have lived in Mexico (where I studied and later returned for many trips) and Senegal (where my daughter was in the Peace Corps from 1998 to 2000). I have been to Senegal many times and met a United Methodist missionary there and we became friends. I moved to Villa Park, Illinois, in the late 1970s. At that time, it was mostly white; some of my neighbors were Polish immigrants and a few were African-Americans. Across North Avenue, whole neighborhoods had changed. Now, in Villa Park, I have noticed that at least thirteen different languages are spoken at the elementary school and the neighborhood is now mostly Hispanic and with some Muslim families.

I grew up in Lathrop, Missouri — population 888, according to the sign at the edge of town. I was an only child, but had a close first cousin. Interesting to note, prior to 1918, Lathrop was known as the mule capital, as it raised stock for U.S. wars, and my father was involved in mule transportation. My family moved to Lathrop in 1944 and my earliest memories are of my childhood friends: a girl down the street (I do not remember her name) and two boys, Gene Stout and Steve Kidd, who was African-American and who my mother never let in the house. Another interesting note, Steve Kidd is the father of famous NBA player Jason Kidd.

As for my mother, she was a "foreigner" — she grew up twenty-five miles down the road. My father's parents and brother were founders of the Methodist church in town. The town used to be a Civil War watering stop along the railroad. As for my formal education, I have a bachelor's degree from the University of Missouri, a bachelor's degree in foreign trade from the Thunderbird Graduate School, and a master's degree in clinical psychology from Wheaton College; and I have trained in the field of family therapy, which I enjoyed the most.

Currently, I am an ESL tutor at the PRC, but I began volunteering in 2010 after my retirement in 2009. My old office happened to be right across the way from the PRC and I could see it from my window. I started with an orientation open house on tutoring and then received an email a couple of days later. When I responded, I think thirty seconds later I received two emails asking me if I could teach ESL and if I could start tomorrow. Since then, I have been helping two nights a week! While I tutor at a couple of other places, I find the variety of people at the PRC to be fantastic. We have a smattering of eastern Europeans, people from Mexico, Syria, Mongolia, China, Japan, the Ivory Coast, and more.

My favorite experience with the PRC is not having to see people again because they have graduated and gotten a job. That is the measure of success for this program. When someone can come in and carry on a conversation or tell a joke in English — that is my favorite thing.

One of the more difficult aspects of working here is trying to get through to people with *no* understanding of the language and who have *no* support. Also, dealing with situations where someone may be homeless (or virtually so) or with the elderly when they are isolated. Other difficulties arise when adult children who have previously emigrated are in the process of trying to petition their family members in — particularly their parents. Currently, the process for Mexicans can take up to fifteen years and, in the case of the Philippines, sometimes longer. This puts extra stress on the situation. On the other end of the spectrum, we sometimes work with people who are good productive members of society who are here without documents or "legal status" and I feel bad about the nasty things that could happen to them — I think I worry about that the most.

I do not know if this is my proudest moment at the PRC, but I was recently helping a young nineteen-year-old man from Mexico who has only been here two months. The last time I was here with him, he was working on a poem and he was able to read an entire stanza of the poem. That's incredible.

I am working on having some friends volunteer for the food pantry at the Wheaton facility, and I am working on a friend of mine to volunteer at the Westmont facility, but he is involved with the church right now. I wish that I could get more people involved, but my children are both ESL teachers and my wife works with Meals on

Wheels. By the way, she was the one who recruited me to volunteer here.

One of the things that I think can help make the PRC more visible is to get the word out among other like-minded charitable organizations and churches in the local area. This can open up other ways to get donations and volunteers involved.

❑

Lukas Rodriguez

Interviewed, Spring 2014

Editors' note: Lukas is a longterm volunteer and former PRC board member. He won the "Volunteer Service Award in 2012 for the northeastern Illinois region," after being nominated by the PRC literacy staff "for outstanding work as a computer instructor and literacy tutor, including coordination of classes such as computer instruction in Spanish, GED, and financial literacy."

I grew up in Chile. In my family, I was the oldest sibling of two sisters and a brother. We used to live in a small city at the end of the world, close to the place where the Pacific Ocean meets the Atlantic Ocean. It is called "Punta Arenas," that translates to something like "Point of Sand." Even though it was cold most of the year and freezing cold in winter and even though the family was moving frequently inside town, making it hard to make friends, life was fun. Our main responsibility was school, once done with the school tasks we enjoyed a great amount of freedom and open spaces. The weekends and vacation time were the best; we were able to wander in the nearby forests, lakes, and sea shores for long hours. Every day was a new adventure. The most memorable event was a four-months-long road trip, crossing the southern part of Argentina and the long geography of Chile, which took us to the opposite side of the country. That was memorable because we were able to get to know the country and to contact all our relatives, many of them who were unknown to us until then.

Two years before I started the university, Augusto Pinochet [the president of Chile who overthrew the elected government of Salvador Allende in 1973 and remained president till 1990] had become the ruler of the country by a military coup. The dictator made life very hard for 50 percent of the Chilean people. The economy was horrible, but from the outside, Chile looked well off, an economic boom. However looking at the UN report for the past decades, Chile had been traditionally part of the ten countries in the world with the worst distribution of wealth. Pinochet just continued this tradition in the name of free markets. During my time at the university I took part in the student movement, joining frequent protests. The main demand was to gain some democracy back, to get the human rights to be respected, but police brutality was the norm. Anyone complaining about the situation was a "terrorist," providing them with the excuse to jail people, to beat then, and in some cases "disappearing" or killing people. We could not understand the United States support for Pinochet, considering it was the role model for democracy.

From that time, a particular experience is worth sharing; it was during vacation time from the university, we were traveling north (hitchhiking) with some friends, going to visit a famous poet's place of birth. After a couple of days of traveling, we got there and camped close to the town, on the base of a mountainous area (4,000 meters high). It was a special place because of its beauty. The mountains around were huge and impressive. I used to do a lot of climbing middle-size mountains and this was an opportunity not to be missed. Then the next day, early in the morning, I left the camp by myself and started climbing one of the nearby mountains. It took five hours to reach the peak doing soft climbing. Although the peak was covered in snow, the view was amazing, the air super clear and refreshing, it was a spiritual experience. Around 4 P.M. it was time to go back, unfortunately, I ended up very far away from my camp site and it was late afternoon already. Trying to reach the camp before it got dark I started to hitchhike to get back to my friends. It took some time for a car to pass by, but finally one stopped. It was a civil police car, although the driver and co-driver said nothing, I learned that later. I had been in the wilderness for several days, I appeared grungy, with ratty hair and a growing beard, nothing pleasant to view or smell. When the car was passing close to my camp, I requested them to drop me off and thanked them for the ride, but the driver told me he was police and he was detaining me because he suspected I was on "drugs." Funny thing how my spiritual journey brought me to jail. I was held there for three days; I didn't get a glass of water nor food and I was constantly beaten by the police, and threatened with being disappeared or killed. It was a scary experience, and there was no basis to their allegation. Every day I was taken to a circle of armed police to be questioned and beaten. You could see they were just having fun and abusing their power. I had been away from my family for several years already. I was nobody and nobody knew where I was, in an unknown town in the middle of nowhere, certainly an easy target.

Fortunately for me, my friends had gotten a tip that I had been taken by the civil police and placed in jail. They started asking questions about my whereabouts with the authorities. I believe their effort saved my life, because at that point I was becoming convinced I was done for. You try to convince yourself that this kind of thing happens to some "people," like "criminals" or "terrorists," but not to regular and law-abiding citizens. It is hard to believe the police are doing these kinds of things because in our society you grow up with an image of cops as protectors. It was a shocking and scary awakening.

I got married in 1985 to Isabel, a beautiful and caring young lady. We had been dating for three years already. Because of a good offer in Puerto Rico, I traveled there to complete a four-months internship in a computer company. Once the internship had ended, a Puerto Rican University asked me to stay and fill a teaching position in computer science. They offered $1,000 a month! It was unbelievable! In Chile, the average salary was around $80 a month. It never was on my mind to leave Chile, but reviewing the facts, I decided this was a great opportunity for the family we were starting. Half a year later Isabel moved to Puerto Rico with me.

In contrast to Chile under the dictatorship, with repression, lack of opportunities, and a state of mind where everybody trusted nobody, Puerto Rico was relaxed with year-long summers and very warm people. Some of our best memories will be forever linked to Puerto Rico. All of my kids were born there: they completed preschool and elementary school in a very friendly environment, doing a lot of sports. After five years we were allowed to become U.S. citizens! That was special because it removed the uncertainty about the future that we were facing every year.

After thirteen years in Puerto Rico, it was time to explore new opportunities. I was lucky to be accepted at an American company and quickly moved to the United States. Jumping from Puerto Rico to the United States was easy; because Puerto Rico is considered part of the United States. A friend helped the family to get the accommodations required to survive in the United States. She provided us orientation to navigate this new culture in America. In Chile and Puerto Rico you can get by using public transportation to get anywhere. In the United States, because nothing is within a good walking distance, and public transportation is limited, a car was a must. At my new job as an IT engineer, I always found people willing to help, in particular because of my limitations with the language. I'm grateful because of that. There were instances of bad experiences, but very few.

Coming here, the biggest cultural shock for Isabel and me was the language. In Chile, the school system did teach us a very basic British English. Faced with the American English, it was a shock on two fronts: it sounded so different and used so much slang. At the beginning we could not make out a word of what the people were saying; they appeared to speak so fast that we could not differentiate one word from the other. It made it very difficult to communicate for us. It took, at least for me, five years living in the United States to be more comfortable speaking in non-technical English. In comparison, we were amazed how fast our kids learned the language: six months in the United States and they were able to communicate; one year later and they were swimming like fishes in the language.

Today my kids are grown up. All of them are warm, happy, and caring people; that is what made us proud more than anything. One son is studying for an MBA; the second son completed a BA on film production and is planning to explore opportunities in Hollywood (although he has made more money as a swimming coach…so far). One daughter gave us our first grandson; she delayed her studies in child care to attend to her son. Finally, the second daughter is completing a degree in architecture.

One of the most cherished experiences for me was becoming a U.S. citizen and being able to vote! It didn't result in my candidate going to the White House, but it was great feeling anyway. In this regard I cannot avoid thinking back to Chile and my people. A lot of things have changed there: Pinochet is gone and democracy is back! For the last twenty years Chile has had a democratic government with elections every four years. The economy is booming, and the distribution of wealth is improving.

I became involved with the People's Resource Center because at that time the director of the Computer Program was a person of great vision. He was looking for volunteers to teach the basics of computers to Spanish-speaking clients. It was an opportunity to do what I loved the most: to teach and to help people who I feel part of, that's why I developed the first Spanish computer program. A lot of changes have happened along the way: today the PRC at St. Paul Lutheran Church has grown with more instructors and is able to provide to the Spanish community multiple services: computers, GED, English, and, from time to time, special workshops on financial literacy, domestic violence, and immigration.

The experiences that I have had at the PRC have been remarkable. The People's Resource Center has become a place where the Hispanic clients are developing a sense of community. The clients that we work with, made friends with each other, form relationships with one another, help each other to solve problems and to find information on so many topics; it has become more than just a classroom. When people begin their experience at the PRC many of them feel lonely and they are very insecure; along the way you can see how they became more and more confident. This is more evident with women, who tend to be the majority of our Hispanic clients. Before coming to the United States their traditions forced them to stay at home as a wife and mother. Along the way many of them had been exposed to different types of abuses that break your heart; for them the classroom holds a special meaning; they are the ones who benefit the most and through them their families.

Because an important segment of our Hispanic clients came from rural areas, they are coming with a very basic foundation in terms of language skills and their experience of urban life is limited. For them, the United States is not only a big change in terms of the language, it is a cultural shock in every possible aspect of their life: ideas, activities, things, gadgets, social responsibilities, legal framework, etc. Everything is new and the amount of information is overwhelming. This limited exposure to urban life and in particular American urban life, leads often to bad economic decisions and they tend to be easy prey of any possible money scam. That is why, as a PRC volunteer at Saint Paul, as part of GED, computer and English courses, we made extra efforts to provide them with all kinds of information and workshops on topics ranging from diet, financial literacy, domestic violence, immigration, and taxes.

Success is hard to define; you provide the clients a new tool that could open for them new opportunities, but these tools and knowledge open a door for new problems too. Great! You learned computing and now you have a computer too… uhm…, but you got a virus, backups, bad hardware, or a lot of useless information that is hard to navigate. These scenarios, if not handled properly, can be very confusing and frustrating for the clients. The great satisfaction for us as volunteers is that a student starts making relevant use of what he/she is learning and by doing that gets more confident and more independent. It happens when a client who is learning English finally is able to communicate, when a woman decides she is better off getting out of an abusive relationship, when a client in the computer program starts using it to reach and reconnect with remote family or to find relevant information that allows them to solve day to day problems; that is success!

On a practical note: PRC's GED program at St. Paul Lutheran has been able to help fifteen students to pass the GED exam, and several of them are pursuing college studies!

The PRC is creating and empowering a community that goes beyond the classroom.

❑

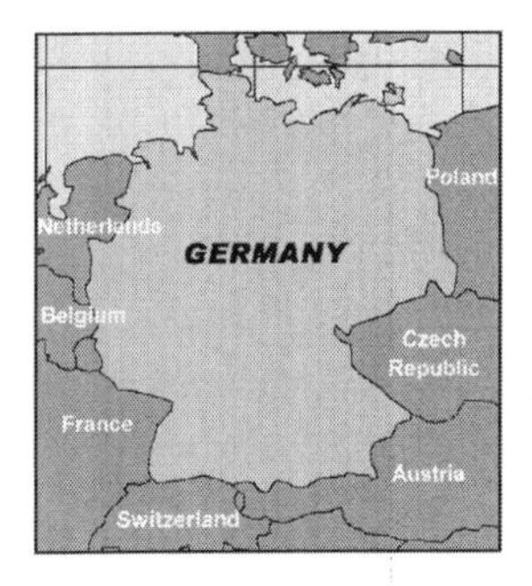

Margaret Paulus Roth

Interviewed, Spring 2014

> *Editor's (interviewee) note:* After interviewing and editing the stories for this book, I decided to share my childhood history, because I could identify with many of the situations that the people shared with us: living under a dictatorship that did not allow any freedom of speech or assembly and tortured and killed Jews and other minorities; becoming an internal refugee; being bombed; and experiencing extreme cold and hunger. However, there is one difference from the stories of the interviewees: the conditions in Germany were temporary and didn't last into my teenage years, while many of the interviewees were trapped in an endless loop of poverty, abuse, war, and discrimination.

I was born in Stuttgart during the Nazi years in Germany, one year before World War II broke out. My childhood was generally happy, however at times it was very sad. When my father was drafted into the war I was one year old, and he didn't come back from the war until I was three. My family and I lived in an apartment house with twelve other families. The house was a microcosm of German society at that time. Some of those with whom we lived among were anti-Nazi, some pro-Nazi supporters, and an elderly Jewish couple, just to name a few. I had no concept of people being different, or that just being Jewish meant being branded, imprisoned, tortured, or brutally murdered. I did not know until after the war that two sisters who lived in the apartment across from the Jewish couple would spit on them when they met them. (The Jewish couple managed to emigrate in 1943.) My parents were part of a Catholic academic youth group that was disbanded by Goebbels [Minister for Propaganda of the Third Reich, one of closest and most feared allies of Hitler] because of their anti-Nazi philosophy, but they continued to meet secretly in our apartment.

I don't remember much before 1943 when I was five. At that time, the bombing raids became very severe in my area. In 1944 the whole town was completely destroyed. There were many aspects of our way of life that I do remember in detail. One was the fact that we would always sleep with all our clothes on. Living on the fourth floor of the apartment building we never knew when we would have to run to the cellar at a moment's notice during an air raid. We always had to be ready. At times due to the bombing raids my family and the others had to sleep in the hallways to be away from the windows. There were many instances, after a raid, of unexploded bombs in the streets. For days we would be unable to go outside, because we had to wait for the people to come and dismantle the unexploded bombs. Outside every apartment's door was a bucket of water because if a bomb hit the house there were people who were trained to take the bomb and put it in the water so that it would become harmless, although I never saw this happen.

Every family had two cellars and an attic; the houses were all built very well. My family's potato cellar became the bunker for the whole house. All the people in the building would run down to the cellar and stay; every so often they would send a man up to see if it was clear or not and we could all leave the bunker. We were very lucky that our house never got completely destroyed. However, a bomb came through the roof, the fifth floor apartment, into our apartment, and lodged itself in an easy chair, but did not explode.

At this time, 1943, it was clear to everyone in Germany, except Hitler, that Germany was losing the war. He ordered all women and children to evacuate the big cities and go to live with relatives in rural areas. If you had no relatives to live with, you would be assigned living accommodations. My mother called a stepbrother of my grandmother, who already had nine kids, and they said right away "come" and they would find us somewhere to stay. My mother had called other relatives, who turned us down, even though they had ample space for us to live. When we got to my grandmother's stepbrother we were offered one room in their carpentry shop. Due to these living arrangements, I can really identify with homelessness. For two years my family lived in one room in the house with a family of eleven. We had less than enough food, and there was no running water in the building. Two large clothes closets were brought from our apartment in Stuttgart, behind them were the beds, in front were our living quarters with an easy chair, four kitchen chairs, and a small table . In the meantime, my father had been discharged from the army because his father had been killed in World War I and was allowed to stay in Stuttgart and work. He worked for a huge insurance company, but at this time there was no insurance being sold. His job was to look after the building and keep inventory of the destruction and order repairs after bombing raids. On the weekends my father would leave the city to visit us.

We had to pump all our water and carry it up a flight of stairs. We used an electric coil in a pot of water to boil all of our water for cooking. As kids we were able to go outside all the time. However, once there was a flood in the cellar of the house and the parents were all concerned that we would have even less food to eat. The flood water ruined all the potatoes and other vegetables that they had stored there. This made everyone so desperate. As kids we loved the flood water though; we would take a little bath tub and float and paddle around in it.

At the end of the war the intense hunger started. It lasted for about three years, and we all suffered greatly. This is why when I hear of people being hungry I just cannot stand it, because I have suffered severe prolonged hunger. We were allotted a loaf of bread a week for five people and lived basically on vegetables, potatoes, and millet mush. On occasion we would get some butter, and when we did get it there were options: either we could put the butter into the millet mush to let it soak into the whole bowl so that all tasted a little better, or just eat one spoonful of the mush with the butter, which tasted great. The cold was also horrible since we had only wood fires. Coal and wood could only be purchased with ration cards, and they never seemed to last the whole month.

In 1944 while we were living in this village I remember looking over in the direction of Stuttgart and seeing the crimson sky and my mother saying over and over, "Will dad survive this?" This was when the city was bombarded by the Allied planes and leveled. My father did survive.

Months before the Americans came to liberate our village, they flew in low-flying planes through our valley and shot at everything that moved. My mother had to take her mother-in-law to the doctor, nine miles away. Since by that time, public transportation had completely shut down, they walked to the next city. On the way back, they were surprised by the Allied planes and ducked behind bushes or houses as soon as they heard them in the distance.

In May 1945 the Americans came to our village. And they rolled in with jeeps and tanks and everyone was just amazed at the sight. Before they arrived, we had all been given little bags, into which we put dried fruit, a flashlight, and other items, and then we were told where to run into the woods and where to meet. I was in charge of my four-year-old brother, and we were to run away when the Americans came to the village. Actually, when they came we ended up in a bunker and my mother who was an English teacher wrote a sign at our room door, saying, "Please do not hurt us I have three kids." After we left the bunker, the Americans went from house to house in search of weapons. When they came to our house they talked a bit to my mother; they said they were not here to hurt us but to rescue all of us from Hitler's rule. My mother was touched by this.

We knew the Americans had a lot of stuff. The neighborhood kids had a great idea. We sent my two-year-old brother to beg the U.S. soldiers for candy. And he got a lot of it. When we brought it back to our parents they threw it in the creek behind the house. They did not trust the Americans. We were so upset at our parents, so we went back and got more candy, but never told our parents; we all survived quite well. Hitler had built the autobahn to move his troops and a stretch was close to our village. The Americans rode on it and threw their food rations to the people lined up on the roadside. Germans were just so hungry at this time.

Before the Americans came, my parents listened to foreign radio, which was strictly prohibited under the Nazis. Twice my parents were visited by the Gestapo. Once they ransacked the apartment, going through every single thing we owned. Every piece of paper was looked at, every single drawer was opened. My parents had hidden a list of addresses of the group that had been disbanded by Goebbels in the false bottom of the grandfather clock. If the list had been found my parents would have been put in prison. My mother said only two things about this incident, "The Gestapo people were really stupid" and "I was sweating the whole time they were there."

When we went back to Stuttgart I was almost seven. After the war I was severely underweight and the U.S. agency CARE took forty kids from Stuttgart who were malnourished and sickly and paid for us to go to Switzerland for three months. I was chosen. My host family spoiled me rotten. In 1948 there was a lot of resentment of Germans, but the woman I lived with was a widow and she and her adult children gave me three wonderful months. When I was living with my host mother I began to become healthier and when I came back to Germany I had chocolates, sweaters, sausages, and many other things that we could not get in Germany then. Everyone in Switzerland was so hospitable to me and I was able to bring everything through customs without being searched. After the war, American CARE packages arrived with yellow peanut butter that looked like chocolate squares. They were very high in protein and we would have to eat them at school. I hate to say it, but I disliked them immensely. I still hate peanut butter and cannot stand the smell of it.

I went to Africa during my years at the university. This is where I learned what real poverty was, permanent poverty. As Germans, we knew that when the war was over we would be better off. Yes, we were hungry, but we knew times were going to change eventually. However, many in Africa just never get out of poverty.

I did experience hunger, cold, and homelessness and that's why when Dorothy McIntyre started the PRC, I knew I wanted to be part of it. I have volunteered in one way or other since its beginnings. Listening to the stories of the people involved with the PRC made me relive some of my memories and I was shocked to see that governments and some citizens still make lives of some people miserable and intolerable.... I would love to help them all to get to the United States and to receive the great services of the PRC.

❑

Reflections

The life experiences you have read throughout this book do not need explanation or embellishment, but they do invoke reactions. Those of us who have the privilege of working and volunteering at People's Resource Center understand these reactions and have found that in sharing them we are often broadening perspectives of those around us and making the world feel just a bit smaller. So often, volunteers share that they receive so much more from their interactions with PRC's clients than they feel they are contributing. The following are reflections that the editors and the student interviewers felt compelled to share with you, the readers. Perhaps you too will have reflections of your own. Please considering sharing them by visiting WWW.PEOPLESRESOURCECENTER.ORG and clicking "Contact Us" at the top of the page.

The Editors

Margaret: Imagine arriving at O'Hare Airport and not being able to understand the announcements or to read the signs because you did not know a word of English. Now imagine arriving at the airport and not being able to read the signs because you do not know any English, but you also have never learned to read or write — in any language. This is the situation with many refugees who had to leave their countries for various reasons, won the lottery to come to the United States, and have been assigned to Chicago.

We interviewed many who were in this situation, but they did not allow themselves to be victims. They decided to do something about their lack of education, their lack of knowledge about the American culture, and their lack of technical or professional skills to land a job. They found that they had come to the right place, where help was available. They were not stopped by their ethnic or religious or political backgrounds from receiving services. These services were there for the asking. And they took the opportunities; they retrained and educated or reeducated themselves. They began to learn to read and write, and then pursued a GED or college degree, and studied for citizenship.

The PRC played a huge role in their quest because, while they were studying, they could also use the food pantry, the clothes closet, and the computer classes, and they could learn to write a résumé in order to find a job.

The stories show that with a bit of understanding and some help, immigrants and refugees can lead full and productive lives despite the hardships and setbacks they faced in their home countries. What they are asking for is to be given a chance and for us to be patient when they struggle with English and the subtleties of American culture.

Warren: Getting to know your neighbor is not boring. Every life is unique. No two persons have the same experiences over a lifetime. As Margaret and I interviewed and edited the interviews done by the students, the fact became clearer that each individual — regardless of age, gender, or country of origin — had her or his own compelling story. There were similarities that allowed us to group the stories into segments, but no two stories were the same.

One of the most important reflections I have on the interviews in this book is the candor of the people being interviewed. Regardless of the age, gender, or ethnic background of the interviewer, those who sat across the table were willing to disclose intimate and often emotional incidents of their lives without fear or reserve. I asked myself a number of times, "Would I have told another person what I just heard?" Though in most cases the interviewees had just met the student who was writing down or recording their stories, the experiences recounted were obviously straight from the heart. My only explanation for this level of candor was the fact that we were at the People's Resource Center and those being interviewed felt that they could trust anyone who represented the PRC.

You cannot tell from looking at a person what hardships he or she has suffered in the course of a lifetime. It is only when you have a face-to-face conversation with a person willing to tell the story that you get the full impact of what that person has gone through. For me that was one of the most enduring lessons that I learned from this exercise. I feel that those who related their life experiences made my life more complete because I could empathize with them in the context of their own reality rather than just in my imagination.

Student Interviewers

The Benedictine University History Department Students:
Seniors: Chris Cabellero, Victoria Harwood (Scholars Program), Sadia Mohiuddin, Jason Vitell
Sophomore: Rachel Jones

In general, all the students felt that they had learned a great deal about the home countries of the people they interviewed. They also thought that they should have been able to do research on each of these countries prior to their interviews. They expressed surprise that some of those they were interviewing wanted to go back to their home countries despite the sufferings and hardships they had experienced there.

Even though a few of the students interviewed people who became emotionally upset, to the point of tears, they came to view the interviewees' accounts as success stories as they found out what life in the United States has meant to them. The students all realized that the experiences they heard were only part of much more extensive stories. They adhered, however, to their initial instructions not to press those interviewees who became upset for more details than they were willing to disclose.

The following excerpt from the written reflections of the student interviewers are divided into three categories: Perceptions of Immigrants and Refugees; Perceptions of the People's Resource Center; and Comments on Individual Interviews

Perceptions of Immigrants and Refugees

Rachel: "Once you have listened to their stories previous judgments are forgotten.... I feel as though this project has forced me to grow into a better understanding of people who are different than me.... This person that you just spent an hour with does not know you, but you know them perhaps better than their best friend knows them."

Victoria: "Even though two of the people I interviewed were from the same country, they had two very different experiences.... I did not realize how hard it was to move from your home country and start a new life in a country where one doesn't know the language or does not have the money or resources to truly prosper.... I never knew how common it was for the government to split up families.... I am much more open-minded to hearing the concerns of immigrants."

Chris: "These stories prove that the world is still a harsh and unrelenting place. But with hope in that there is a place of solitude, freedom can and will be achieved. For me, being born and raised in a middle-income family, I had no idea that these types of stories existed."

Sadia: "Before this internship started, I never realized the importance of the basic necessities of life.... Talking to some of the people taught me that you have to believe in yourself and work hard to get what you want. You cannot accept help from others without helping yourself first.... The project was a true life-changing experience; not only did I meet amazing people, but I learned about different countries all over the world."

Jason: "Like most Americans, I do not see the distinctions between the many Middle Eastern (or Muslim) nations and cultures. I, like most, tend to lump them all together and concoct some amalgamation of cultural, ethnic, and religious caricatures as filtered through the national news media.... What I learned from the stories is that the fishbowl of my life is nothing compared to what some of these people have gone through or experienced.... This internship was a good reminder that seeing a person for who they actually are should not be limited to what they look like or where they are from."

Perceptions of the People's Resource Center

Rachel: "The PRC helps those who are having difficulties making ends meet.... The PRC helps people build relationships and makes them feel more at home no matter from how far away they came to get to where they are today."

Sadia: "When I first got to the Center, I was really nervous, but then I noticed that most of the staff members had big smiles on their faces and were very welcoming.... The PRC has changed my view on how I see the world, and has made me want to volunteer and try to help people change their lives for the better.... I like that it's open to everyone from everywhere; the staff doesn't judge you."

Jason: "It should also be noted that every interviewee praised not only the existence of the PRC, but the patience and kindness of the staff.... Just by knowing the language, these people are now able to better interact with people they encounter on the street."

Comments on Individual Interviews

Victoria: "Although all the people I interviewed did have similarities, their stories were all unique.... It was still clear that the United States has made slow progress in getting children reconnected with their families.... A parent wants to do all they can do for their children even if it means leaving them behind in order to provide for them.... It was because of their reactions to stories, both good and bad, that I knew they were telling the truth. Most of the stories were not pleasant, so I do not feel as if they would fabricate the stories."

Chris: "Every story was different and entailed an adventure with devastation and hope.... All of the stories that were told eventually had a happy ending.... The hardest part about this experience was being able to relate to the individuals telling the stories, because I have never experienced hardships in this manner."

Sadia: "I found one of the interviewees especially interesting when

[she] told me her family back in Africa doesn't believe her when she tells them that she doesn't have any money to send to Africa, because she has hardly enough for her family here.... After the interview I felt as if I knew her; her story was so powerful and upsetting."

Jason: "My first solo interviewee was as patient with me as I had intended to be with him. After we finished, he told me that he considered himself my friend, and I felt the same." [Another interviewee] "did not have much formal education, but I admired him greatly for taking the leap of faith and coming to a new land without any understanding of the language or any family waiting for him."

❑

Epilogue

Diversity is about all of us, and about us having to figure out how to walk through this world together.
– Jacqueline Woodson, author

The personal stories shared throughout this compilation depict such diversity in experiences, in cultures, in education and languages, yet at the same time also depict remarkable uniformity. Regardless of the originating country, those who have found assistance from People's Resource Center over the years have done so with reasons that match those of countless others. They are seeking hope for a safer tomorrow for their families through healthy food and warm clothing. They are seeking opportunities for a brighter tomorrow by improving their skills and education.

People's Resource Center has, since its beginning in 1975, been welcoming of anyone. In our global society today, I am hard-pressed to think of a single person I know who has no connections to individuals who have come from another land. Perhaps it's a family member who came to the United States years ago. Perhaps it's a classmate of a child who was adopted from another country. Or perhaps, as the preceding stories have illustrated, it's a new neighbor right here in DuPage County.

Last year, 28 percent of the nearly 32,000 clients served at People's Resource Center were immigrants or refugees who came from more than 100 different countries. They are now living in DuPage County and working to make the best possible life for their families.

All of us at People's Resource Center have learned so very much from our experiences with these individuals whom we have the pleasure of assisting every day. I have found myself stunned by the power of the experiences they have endured and am humbled by the courage and determination that has enabled them to share their stories through this book. Many thanks to each and every individual interviewed for willingly sharing such personal stories.

My sincere gratitude goes out to Dr. Vincent Gaddis and the Benedictine University student interviewers who dedicated their time to conducting and compiling the interviews. This publication would not have been possible without the hundreds of hours of work completed by Warren and Margaret Roth, who volunteered their time to pull together all of the details for this book and edited each story, tying them all together with the Preface, Introduction, and Reflections. The Roth's have been dedicated to People's Resource Center and our community since the very beginning and have helped to shape and mold this organization into what it is today.

I hope that in reading these stories, you have found inspiration to welcome diversity into your life in a new way. Our community can become stronger when we embrace the strengths that exist within it. There is so much to learn from our diverse neighbors.

If you'd like to join us at People's Resource Center in the various ways we are working to make a difference, please visit www.PeoplesResourceCenter.org to become a volunteer, make a donation, or simply learn more about our work in the community.

Kim Perez
Executive Director
People's Resource Center